"WHETHER NATALIE GOLDBERG TELLS US ABOUT HER OWN LIFE OR THAT OF HER BELOVED TEACHER, UNDERNEATH HER WRITING THERE IS ALWAYS A *DAKINI* ACCOMPANIMENT, A TINKLING BELL OF UNDERSTATED HUMOR, AND IN THE BASS A GREAT BOOMING DRUM— THIS HEARTBEAT REPRESENTING THE ONLY THING THAT CAN SAVE ANYONE—INTENSE AND PERFECT LONGING."

—Clarissa Pinkola Estés, Ph.D., author of *Women Who Run with the Wolves*

"I want to call up everyone I know and read *Long Quiet Highway* to them over the phone. I want to give it to every writer that I love."

—Ellen Gilchrist, winner of the National Book Award and author of *Net of Jewels*

"This is a beautiful book. Goldberg's writing is gorgeous and brings us closer to the lost years of adolescence. Suddenly, those years became luminous. I moved with her from teacher to teacher and broke open when she met her Zen master."

—Geneen Roth, author of *When Food Is Love*

"If you want to know the heart of a writer and the answer to a Zen master's koan, read this book."

—Jack Kornfield, Buddhist teacher and author of *A Path with Heart*

"*Long Quiet Highway* is the autobiography of a thoughtful woman who grounded herself in Eastern thought and Western art—a precise history of Natalie Goldberg's adventures as poet, teacher, and spiritual student—a book full of sentiment and anecdote."

—Allen Ginsberg

Also by Natalie Goldberg

WRITING DOWN THE BONES

WILD MIND

BANANA ROSE

And look for

LIVING COLOR

Available in
September 1997

LONG QUIET HIGHWAY

Waking Up in America

NATALIE GOLDBERG

BANTAM BOOKS

New York • Toronto • London • Sydney • Auckland

Grateful acknowledgment is made for permission to reprint from the following:
"The Memoirs of Jesse James," copyright © 1970 by Richard Brautigan. Reprinted by
permission of The Helen Brann Agency, Inc.; Excerpt from "The Wanderer Returned" from
Fully Empowered by Pablo Neruda. Translation copyright © 1975 by Alistair Reid,
Reprinted by permission of Farrar, Straus & Giroux, Inc.; No. 22 from "Mountains and
Waters Sutra" from Moon in a Dewdrop: Writings of Zen Master Dogen, edited by
Kazuaki Tanahashi. Copyright © 1985 by the San Francisco Zen Center. Published by North
Point Press and reprinted by permission of Farrar, Straus & Giroux, Inc.; "The Crow That
Visited Was Flying Backwards," copyright © 1984 by John Brandi. Reprinted with
permission of Tooth of Time Books, Inc.; "Simply snow falls" haiku from Inch by Inch.
Reprinted by permission of Tooth of Time Books, Inc.; "Late Fragment" from A New Path to
the Waterfall by Raymond Carver, copyright © 1989 by the estate of Raymond Carver.
Reprinted with permission of Atlantic Monthly Press; Poem by Katagiri Roshi in Wind Bell,
twenty-fifth anniversary issue, copyright © 1986. Reprinted by permission of the San
Francisco Zen Center.

LONG QUIET HIGHWAY

A Bantam Book

PUBLISHING HISTORY
Bantam hardcover edition published March 1993
Bantam trade paperback edition / March 1994

ISBN 0-553-37315-3

Published simultaneously in the United States and Canada

Bantam Books are published by Bantam Books, a division of Bantam Doubleday Dell
Publishing Group, Inc. Its trademark, consisting of the words "Bantam Books" and the
portrayal of a rooster, is Registered in U.S. Patent and Trademark Office and in other
countries. Marca Registrada. Bantam Books, 1540 Broadway, New York, New York 10036.

PRINTED IN THE UNITED STATES OF AMERICA

FFG   0   9   8   7

For my teacher
Dainin Katagiri Roshi
with boundless love, gratitude, and appreciation

Acknowledgments

I wish to thank Jan Best, who once again typed the manuscript from the original handwritten pages; Jean Leyshon, my assistant and also a long-time student of Katagiri Roshi; Kate Green, for being my main reader; John Thorndike, for his initial comments on Part I; Geneen Roth and Laura Davis, who also read Part I; the Minneapolis Public Library, for tracking down the Brautigan poem; Richard Chakrin, an old friend from Mr. Cates's class; Robert Handleman, who lived on my block in Farmingdale; Brett Gadbois, an old friend and early teacher of writing and practice; Tomoe Katagiri and the sangha of the Minnesota Zen Meditation Center, and also the sangha of everyone, wherever you are, and of all things; and Jonathon Lazear, my agent, and Toni Burbank, my editor.

Introduction

There is an order of Buddhist monks in Japan whose practice is running. They are called the marathon monks of Mount Hiei. They begin running at one-thirty A.M. and run from eighteen to twenty-five miles per night, covering several of Mount Hiei's most treacherous slopes. Because of the high altitude, Mount Hiei has long cold winters, and part of the mountain is called the Slope of Instant Sobriety; because it is so cold, it penetrates any kind of illusion or intoxication. The monks run all year round. They do not adjust their running schedule to the snow, wind, or ice. They wear white robes when they run, rather than the traditional Buddhist black. White is the color of death: There is always the chance of dying on the way. In fact, when they run they carry with them a sheathed knife and a rope to remind them to take their life by disembowelment or hanging if they fail to complete their route.

After monks complete a thousand-day mountain marathon within seven years, they go on a nine-day fast without food, water, or sleep. At the end of the nine days, they are at the edge of death. Completely emptied, they become extremely sensitive. "They can hear ashes fall from the incense sticks... and they can smell food prepared miles away." Their sight is vivid and clear, and after the fast they come back into life radiant with a vision of ultimate existence.

I read about these monks in a book entitled *The Marathon Monks of Mount Hiei,* by John Stevens (Shambhala, 1988). It was just before I went to teach the first of four Sunday afternoon

writing seminars at The Loft in Minneapolis. I was excited by
what I read and naturally I wanted to share it. I stood behind
the podium and carried on to fifty Midwestern writers and
would-be writers about how the monks became one with the
mountain they ran on, how they knew the exact time each
species of bird and insect began to sing, and when the moon
rose, the sun set, the wind changed direction.

I was twenty minutes into the seminar's two hours, telling
about the monks, when I looked up and paused. "I guess you
want to know what the marathon monks have to do with
writing?

"Well, they have everything to do with it. The way I see
it, you either break through in your writing—say what you
really need to say—or head for Mount Hiei. As a matter of
fact, take a gun with you next time you go to a café to write.
If you don't connect in your writing that day, just shoot yourself.
Vague writing on Monday—off with the little toe. Tuesday, no
better—the big toe. Get the idea?"

Why do the marathon monks go to such extremes? They
want to wake up. That's how thick we human beings are. We
are lazy, content in our discontent, sloppy, and asleep. To wake
up takes the total effort that a marathon monk can exert. I told
my class on the last day of the four-week seminar, "Well, you
have two choices: Mount Hiei or writing. Which one will you
choose? Believe me, if you take on writing, it is as hard as being
a marathon monk."

There is a story about Hui-k'o, the Second Ancestor of Zen,
who found Bodhidharma in a cave where he was meditating for
nine years. Bodhidharma was the first patriarch, or ancestor, of
Zen in China and, in fact, he brought Zen there from India.

Day and night, Hui-k'o begged Bodhidharma for the teachings. "Please, master, I beseech you. Make my mind peaceful." Bodhidharma ignored him and continued to sit in meditation. This went on for a long time: the beseeching and the ignoring. Then one evening in December, there was a huge blizzard. It snowed all night and all the next day. Hui-k'o just stood outside the cave without moving, until the snow was waist high. He was waiting to be recognized by Bodhidharma. Finally, he took out a knife and cut off his left arm. He threw it in front of Bodhidharma. You can imagine the red blood on the white snow. With this, Bodhidharma looked up and asked what he wanted.

There is another Zen story about a beautiful woman who came to a monastery and wanted to practice. The head monk said, "If you want to join a monastery, first you must get married and raise three children. Then you can come back." She did this and returned years later. She was still refused entry into the monastery. The head monk said she was too beautiful. She would cause trouble for the other monks. She wanted to practice so badly that she went home and scarred her face. This time when she went to the monastery, they let her in.

Are these stories metaphorical or are they true? I believe they are true. There are people burning to realize the truth of existence and these are the extremes they will go to. Why so violent? Is Zen a violent practice? No, no more so than Jesus Christ being pinned to the cross or Abraham taking his son to be sacrificed.

There is a proliferation of writing books in America. They are very popular. People would rather read about how to become a writer than read the actual products of writing: poems, novels, short stories. Americans see writing as a way to break through their own inertia and become awake, to connect with their deepest selves.

Yes, writing can do this for us, but becoming awake is not easy. One must be persistent under all circumstances and it is not always exciting. It is hard. It is a long quiet highway.

Recently, I drove alone from Minneapolis to New Mexico in late December, the darkest time of the year. I had to cross the southern border of Minnesota, drive straight through Iowa, across Kansas, into Oklahoma and Texas. I had to drive through an hour of sleet near Des Moines, past empty fields and funky cafés that said Elvis ate here. I had a great moment listening to Jessye Norman blast out spirituals in her operatic voice on my car stereo, just as I turned a corner on a thin highway in Kansas. The half moon and one evening star were directly in front of me. A train roared by on my right. The moment was over and I was tired, pulling into a Best Western at ten P.M. in the town of Liberty on the Oklahoma border. What I wanted was to love all of this: my weariness, the wind lifting as I got out of the car at the Texaco station.

To love is to wake up. How do we wake up without becoming a marathon monk on Mount Hiei? Well, some of us will have to go to Mount Hiei. There is no other way. The rest of us must work as tellers in banks, drive our children to school, wash the kitchen floor, buy groceries. The marathon monks go all the way to the edge of death, so they may come back and be alive, so they can know gratitude for this moment. We need to wake up when we buy groceries, push the cart down the aisle, see labels, count out change, feel our step on the floor tile. Every moment is enormous, and it is all we have.

About twelve years ago, Chris Pirsig, the son of Robert Pirsig, who wrote *Zen and the Art of Motorcycle Maintenance,* was senselessly murdered near the San Francisco Zen Center. The killers knifed Chris and ran. They did not take a wallet (I don't even know if Chris had one on him). I was sitting a seven-day meditation retreat in Minnesota. It was December. We all knew Chris. Rumors spread quickly during breaks, even though we were supposed to remain silent. We all awaited our teacher's talk that morning. Katagiri Roshi was close to Chris. He would make it all better.

Roshi walked into the meditation hall, bowed, lit incense, sat down. We chanted. Then he spoke: "Human beings have an idea they are very fond of: that we die in old age. This is just an idea. We don't know when our death will come. Chris Pirsig's death has come now. It is a great teaching in impermanence."

The bell was rung. It was the end of the lecture. I was furious. What kind of thing was that to say? How could Roshi be so cruel? I knew he cared about Chris.

Years later, distraught by learning that Katagiri Roshi had cancer, I cried for many weeks. In May, as I drove to the airport in Albuquerque to fly to see him, I suddenly remembered his talk about Chris. His talk had not been cruel. It was brave. He was willing to cut through all sentiment and touch the fundamental truth of impermanence. I appreciated it. What he said then helped my life now.

This is how we learn. Human life is very big. There is no short cut from Minneapolis to New Mexico. My car had to cover every mile. We learn with every cell and with time, care, pain, and love. I'm sure that many times when the marathon monks woke at midnight to prepare to run, they had an urge to go back to sleep, but the path was ahead of them. We, who are not marathon monks, wake up and have the toothbrush before us—brushing our teeth! the great ritual that gets us out of bed—and then we have the blank page in front of us, or the school bus, or the phone ringing. We all must go on down that highway. Our life is the path of learning, to wake up before we die. This book is about that.

PART ONE

Now I'm aware that I alone am in the vast
  openness
   of the sea
And cause the sea to be the sea.

Just swim.
Just swim.
Go on with your story.

Dainin Katagiri Roshi

Taos High School had career day and I was invited to give a talk. My heart goes out to high school kids, so I accepted and drove the hour and a half from Santa Fe. I hadn't been in a high school for years. What surprised me was how scruffy the kids seemed, how much acne they had, how thin and young they were, how uninterested they acted, how much they wanted to know something and be contacted.

I felt like a fool standing in front of them. What could I tell them about "my career"? I told them I'd written some books. The teacher held up the books. I told them I make my living as a writer.

I took a deep breath. Here was something hard and familiar: that time in our lives when we're innocent, tender, and growing, half with our parents and half about to break out, half in pain, half curious, and also scared. I wanted life to make sense for these kids, and even if I didn't believe it did, I wanted them to. Looking at them slouched in their seats, I knew they hurt and were bewildered, but had no context for it. I wanted to give them one.

"You know, I was a nerd in high school," I said. I paused. "Do they use the word 'nerd' now?"

They nodded.

"I didn't know I'd be a writer. I was just bored."

Then I told them about Mr. Clemente, my high school English teacher. One day he switched off the lights above our heads and told us to listen to the rain. My high school had big windows, I told them, and I felt what a blessing it was as I stood in front of this windowless modern classroom. "That's all we had to do—listen to the rain. There wasn't a test or a quiz on rain, on listening, or on cloudy afternoons."

I told the kids in Taos High School that day to trust in what they loved, that you don't know where it will lead you. "The important thing is to love something, even if it's skateboarding or car mechanics or whistling. Let yourself love it completely."

Then I had them do a writing exercise, because how could I keep talking about being a writer? They had to experience it.

"Okay, I'm going to give you a test"—they all moaned— "but the nice thing about this test is that all your answers are right. Each answer begins with 'I remember.'

"I'll give you the first question and then I'll give you an example of what I want. Okay, give me a detailed memory of your mother, an aunt, or your grandmother. And whichever one you pick, be specific. Don't write, 'I remember her,' but 'I remember my Aunt Gladys, or my mother, or my grandmother.' Here's an example from my own life: 'I remember my mother wore Revlon red lipstick and she loved to eat Oreo cookies and the dark crumbs stuck to the corners of her lips.' Okay, now it's your turn. You have three minutes."

When three minutes were up, I gave them the next one. "Give me a memory of sound." And my example: "I remember the refrigerator hummed in the kitchen all summer and was louder than the crickets."

I gave them a third one: "Give me a memory of the color red. You don't necessarily have to mention red in your writing. For instance, if you say tomato, it immediately engenders the color red in the listener's mind."

I gave them a fourth: "Give me a memory, any memory,

of last summer." The fifth: "Give me a time when you were
lonely."

And for the sixth one, I asked for suggestions. They came
up with memories of third grade. They wanted an example from
my third grade.

"I remember I sat in front of the class next to Mary Brown,
the only black girl in the school. We were whispering to each
other and Mrs. Schneider screamed, 'Natalie, would you shut
up!' This startled everyone. I remember her big teeth as she
screamed this and her red lips and the terror I felt in Mary
Brown's body across from me as she tried hard to look like she
was doing her math."

The Taos students nodded and then they wrote. Then they
read aloud.

We said good-bye to each other, and I wished them well.
I left the class and walked down the long corridor lined with
gray lockers. Again, I was that sad girl in high school, hair pulled
straight back in a pony tail, walking lonesome down those halls,
up and down many flights of stairs, going into Latin and algebra
classes, passing rest rooms and janitor storage rooms, lost for a
whole century of my life.

Thank God for that rain out the window and for Mr. Clemente,
who allowed us in ninth grade to listen to it for no reason, in
the middle of the day. That one moment carried me a long way
into my life.

I didn't know it then. At the time, I think, it made me a
little nervous—it was too naked, too uncontrolled, too honest.
I thought it odd. In those days I was watching my step, making
sure I knew the rules, keeping things in control. I wore the

same long, pleated wool skirt every day, blue cardigan sweater, oxford shoes, and carried a brown leather school bag, even while the other girls were wearing makeup, nylons, heels. I never felt that I fit in. I was uncomfortable with the idea of lipstick, mascara, flirting with boys. I hated the idea that I had to have children, that I would be a housewife. Every grown-up female I knew in our neighborhood stayed at home and took care of her family. I thought I had to do that, too. I rebelled, but I turned it in on myself, and instead of feeling the energy that rebellion can produce, I became repressed and felt bland, un-emotional inside. For fear that people would think I was weird —I saw no one around me I could identify with—I tried not to be noticed. I became a nerd. And here was Mr. Clemente who asked me to listen to the rain, to connect a sense organ with something natural, neutral, good. He asked me to become alive. I was scared, and I loved it.

I signed up for his class for all four years of high school. We studied Archibald MacLeish, Dylan Thomas, James Joyce. That was good, but it was the moment of rain that mattered. I was in Mr. Clemente's class when it was announced over the loudspeaker that President Kennedy had just been shot. We all held our breath and watched for Mr. Clemente's reaction. He turned off the lights, sat down at his desk, took off his glasses, leaned his head on the crook of his arm on the big yellow blotter of his teacher's desk, and wept. Donald Miller, whom I knew from third grade and who drew ships in combat in the corners of his math papers and later died in Vietnam, yelled, "Far out." I don't think he meant anything about Mr. Clemente or JFK; he was just nervous and didn't know what else to do. Mr. Clemente lifted his head off the desk, pointed to the door, and said, "Get out." And Donald, as cool as he could be, but ashamed, tried to saunter out the door.

. . .

After *Writing Down the Bones* had been out for two years, I called Mr. Clemente on the phone. It was twenty-two years after I'd left that school. Mr. Clemente had left the school, too. He didn't remember me, how could he? He'd taught thousands of kids since my time.

He said, "I know that book, *Writing Down the Bones*, but I never thought one of my students had written it."

We talked for a while. He had hated Farmingdale, as I had. He said he was protesting Vietnam at the time and the town was full of hawks. I just knew I was unhappy there, that I didn't belong. I didn't know there was any place better; I didn't know why I was not at ease at the school.

I remembered my grandmother making me a chopped liver sandwich on rye for my school lunch and how when I took it out of its aluminum foil in the cafeteria, the kids sitting around me, holding peanut butter and jelly, or Kraft yellow cheese, or baloney sandwiches, yelled, "Ick!" and held their noses. I felt ashamed. That sandwich held my whole heritage. I was a Jew in a school of mostly Irish and Italian Catholics. I put the sandwich back in its foil, stood up, and headed for the girls' room. I was torn between tossing the sandwich in the garbage and purchasing a cellophane-wrapped Drake's crumb cake from the cafeteria woman, who had gray hair in a fine net and wore a white uniform and white sturdy shoes, or going into the bathroom stall and eating my ethnic sandwich, hidden from view. I loved my grandmother's chopped liver, and I chose the stall.

My grandmother also squeezed fresh orange juice for me every morning. I was often late for the bus and ran out of the house toward the bus stop, my jacket open, my grandmother racing after me down the suburban block, clutching her flowered housecoat at the throat, the orange juice precariously balanced in a glass in her outstretched hand, yelling after me, "Natli, drink, drink," and I tried to ignore her and leaped on the yellow bus.

In truth, I adored my fine white-haired grandmother and grandfather, who spoke Yiddish and snored in the bedroom next to mine. Having my grandparents always around gave me a knowledge that things would die. I looked at my grandmother's face. It was wrinkled, and her eyes became rheumy and deeper set as time went on. Her hands were pale, frail, thin. Something I loved would leave me. I knew this and sometimes I wept in my bed at night.

Often I crawled under the covers with my grandmother in the evening and she told me stories about how her family arrived at Ellis Island from Poland when she was three years old and how she hardly had an accent. She told me how she had met my grandfather: Her older sister Dora owned a small delicatessen in Manhattan and a polite, clean, soft-spoken man came in one day. Auntie Dora said to herself, "Now that's the man for Rosie." He took my grandmother on a carriage ride around Central Park. She was married at seventeen.

I asked her to tell this story to me over and over again. Each time she elaborated more. That ordinary moment of man meets woman became mythical to her granddaughter. And indeed it was. It was my lineage. I was the result of that meeting; each time she began the telling with: "Shall I tell you a story? About a glory? How to begin it? There's nothing in it."

As Mr. Clemente and I talked, he suddenly interrupted me. "Wait a minute! I do remember you. You were a thin brown-haired girl. You sat in the third seat, fourth row. Why,

Natalie, I had no idea you cared. In all those years you never said a word to me."

"I was unhappy," I told him.

"I understand," he said on the phone and I'm sure he was nodding.

I was like that. I took things in deeply, but no one ever knew. In fifth grade I was mad for my teacher, Mr. Berke. He was an energetic man who wore a brown suit and loved science. He taught us scientific experimentation: hypothesis, procedure, materials, observation, conclusion. The idea of hypothesis drove me wild. Hypothesis was something you intuited, but until it was proven, it had only the shimmering quality of a mirage. It entered the realm of the religious: a presence you could not touch. But I wanted to touch it. I became the little scientist. I moved right in. I experimented. I boiled water. The water evaporated and disappeared. I held a glass plate above the boiling water. Steam collected on the glass. I had made water into air into water again. I was delighted. I created a conclusion from my hypothesis that a liquid can become a gas and then become a liquid again. I proved that things change. I touched the transitory nature of life.

In Mr. Berke's science class we used microscopes, glass slides, test tubes. At home I walked around with slides, sticking them in the toilet water, having my grandfather breathe on one, always looking for specimens to be examined. I was ever present if someone cut themselves; I could then catch a blood sample to examine magnified. I was mad for science, though my father and sister made fun of me for wanting a microscope for Hanukkah and a chemistry set for my birthday. Girls shouldn't want those things.

Mr. Berke didn't know how crazy I was about the class.

He was blind to my young heart and to what he had opened in it. When he handed back our big reports on the midwestern states, he came to Carol Heitz's paper and said proudly, "Carol received the highest grade in the class, ninety-seven," and he praised her. Then he continued calling out student names and grades and handing back the reports. Finally, after what seemed an interminable amount of time, he called my name: "Natalie." He opened to the first page of the report to announce my grade. "Oh, you got ninety-nine," and he handed me the paper.

At the end of the year when we were promoted to sixth grade, we were put into tracked classes. I was not in 1A, 1B, or 1C, the top tracks. Mr. Berke placed me in 2A, Mr. Nolan's class, the average group, where we spent the year making Ivory soap sculptures of the Parthenon and Mr. Nolan continually tripped over my school bag as he paced the aisles.

On the last day of Mr. Berke's class when I was handed my fifth-grade report card and the letter saying I was promoted to 2A, I went home weeping. I sat in the sunken living room of our split-level house across from my grandmother and mother on the couch, me on the old, reupholstered stuffed chair, a chasm of brown carpet between us, and cried because I wouldn't be able to learn a foreign language in 2A. My grandmother and mother were bewildered. Why would anyone want to know anything besides English anyway?

The teachers I loved in school were Mr. Clemente, Mr. Berke, and Mr. Cates. Mr. Cates taught a special literature class my junior and senior years of high school. I can't remember what it was called. What I do remember is we read *The Ballad of the Sad Café, The Brothers Karamazov, Crime and Punishment*. Mr. Cates sat on top of a student desk, his feet on the attached wooden chair, his chin in his hand, and asked us a "big" question, "Who would you rather be—Dmitri or Alyosha in the *Brothers*?" and we would discuss this for days. "What is desire?" he asked us after we read a Tennessee Williams play, and my young heart leaped at what I was invited to explore. I jumped from one idea to another, trying to decide what desire was. I thought there was an answer, and that it could be known without experience. I didn't know it then that you only discover desire in the flame of it, only know love when loving.

What I adored in Mr. Cates's class was the opportunity to talk, not just myself, but as a whole class, to have a discussion. Someone said something, another person disagreed or elaborated, and all our minds were free, thoughts were free and equal. You had a mind and you thought. You had a right to form the nebulous energy racing through you into words, to form those words with tongue, teeth, jaws, lips, to move your mouth and speak. This might seem elementary. I'm not talking about high-level debate. I'm talking about a scrawny brown-haired girl whose braces had just been taken off her teeth, who sat in a big public school classroom and was suddenly sprung to life. Her mind and feelings had a voice and she spoke words into the empty space between herself and Mr. Cates, and for her every word—even "the" and "any"—were huge. I'd never had a discussion before, especially about something intangible. At home we discussed what we would have for dinner, or if I was warm enough when I went out in the morning, or what clothing did not fit and would be returned to Abraham and Strauss. My family cared about the given, the concrete: peas, lamb chops, a sale at Macy's, a sore throat, a beautiful face, strong legs, the ring of a phone, the neighbor knocking at our door.

At a large extended family dinner I once asked, hoping to initiate a discussion, "Why did Hitler kill so many Jews? Where was God?" We were studying World War II in history class. My relatives turned to me. They were happy just a moment ago, being together and eating my grandmother's chicken. Why did I have to bring that up? My father, like their great knight, replied, "He hated them and there is no God." That settled it. They all nodded. My grandmother offered me another breast, my favorite, and I accepted it. Meanwhile, I sank into a loneliness that isolated me from words for that loneliness. No God? Hatred? What was hatred? I wanted to examine it, as we did in Mr. Cates's class. Could I hate like that? What caused it? Does my grandmother hate? Does my father, my mother? If someone, an uncle, a cousin, had turned to me, seen into my heart just then, and said, "Why, Natalie, you're lonely," there would have been a great relief. That nontangible, isolated state would have been named and then my lonely existence would have become conscious. But that didn't happen. On many occasions I was told, "You think too much. It will get you in trouble." Thought was useless. You couldn't eat it or buy it. Finally, it was like God. It didn't really exist.

But I had discovered in school that thought had energy. I became excited in Mr. Cates's class. I said words and became alive. I spoke, and with speech I rose out of the suburban ashes like a phoenix. I flew. I soared—for a few minutes anyway—and then sank back into the stupor I was so used to.

Where were the women teachers? Remember the times: the fifties and early sixties. There was only one, a Madame Dujac, straight out of France, whom I liked and remember. She stood with her hands under her armpits in a buttoned light blue cardigan, her swaying breasts held in by a full slip. She demanded that we know her language. (I had advanced from Mr. Nolan into the honors program and could take French.) We memorized Guy de Maupassant. I learned the words, but I did not get the accent or the pronunciation. I thought if it was r you pronounced it like the r in river; I said each letter as I knew it in English. My Brooklyn accent seemed to become stronger in French. Every time I spoke her language, Madame Dujac shook her head violently, which swung her long pearl-earringed lobes back and forth, and she pursed her lips. I tried. I could see and understand the words, but I could not read them aloud.

What excited me about Madame was her energy, her love of French, her urgency to make us, these little savages, this all-girl class from hicktown Farmingdale, learn the music, the depth, the beauty of her native language. And if not that, we should at least not sound like complete fools.

How did she end up among us anyway? A real live French-woman in suburban Farmingdale? I didn't know. Once she said, in French, "Excusez moi, je dois aller aux toilettes," and bolted out the door. I nudged Mary Ellen in front of me. "What'd she say?" Donna, sitting to my right, intercepted my question and answered loudly, "She has to pee." The class giggled. I sat there slightly amazed. You mean, Madame Dujac had to go to the bathroom? She had human functions? She was so exotic to me, I had trouble imagining her as a regular person. In those days, all teachers were in the nonhuman category, but Madame, es-pecially, was a completely foreign breed. Nothing I could emulate.

I heard years later that my father knew her husband. He often came into my father's Aero Tavern and ordered beer and thick pastrami sandwiches. He was a visiting scientist at the Republic Aviation plant nearby. He told my father that Madame could not believe the immaturity of the high school students she taught.

Once in class I accidentally said, "Je suis française." I meant to say, "I *speak* French," not "I *am* French," but that was too much for her, that I dared express, even accidentally, that I was French. She had a ruler in her hand. She pushed out her lips as though about to kiss the air, whipped the stick in circles above her head, and charged at me.

"You are not French. You are not French," she said in perfect English, breaking the strict rule of "only French spoken in this class."

I was quick that morning: "Je sais! Je sais!" I yelled out. She froze near the window, catching herself in midswing, and saw what she was up to; the whole class, including Madame, broke down laughing in huge relief.

"Na-ta-lee," she said in a sweeping staccato, "someday you will come visit me in Paris." I was delighted, but I knew that was ridiculous. I had the great fortune to live near New York City. My aunt Rachel told me, "After New York, there is no place else to go." My family orbited the Big Apple, driving to the Bronx, to Brooklyn, even a few times dipping down to New Jersey, and once or twice heading for the Catskills, always near, though rarely actually going into that great celestial island, Manhattan. No, no reason to go to Paris. We had New York. I would probably never travel as far as that. It was beyond my imagination, but I was flattered that Madame invited me to her hometown, and I nodded my head and smiled.

Mr. Berke loved science; Mr. Clemente, literature; Mr. Cates, thinking; Madame Dujac, French. Each one of them planted a seed and I honor them for it. But some of the other teachers had their effect, too—not always because they were good teachers.

It was Mr. Moscowitz's first year of teaching. He wore a plaid suit, was short, and had terrible facial acne. His only crime was he could not control the class. Control was everything. Mr. Moscowitz didn't carry authority in his body, so it didn't matter that he asked you to sit down. You wouldn't, and you didn't believe his threats about being sent to the principal or being suspended, because too many other kids were out of their seats, grabbing for yellow hall passes and throwing chalk.

Mr. Moscowitz's pimples became the target of our rebellion. We said he was ugly to his face; we grabbed books out of his hands; we flung spitballs at him. We egged each other on to further acts of daring. We crossed into the area of the forbidden. We were rude, obnoxious, violent. Our fervor came from our rage, not so much toward Mr. Moscowitz, though his flagrant acne was frightening to our eighth-grade sensibilities—it mirrored our own faces and our own fears—but toward the public school. Mr. Moscowitz was a chink in the tight school structure. We accepted hall passes, hall monitors, late passes, and school bells as part of the system, but give us a moment to break out and we did. Nancy Vogelsberger was the only one who stood up for Mr. Moscowitz. She wore a white Peter-Pan-collared blouse, a gray skirt, and sturdy shoes. Her brown hair had received a permanent so many times that it looked almost gray and frizzled flat out from the sides of her head. She shook her head and thought we were shameful. We called her the nun.

The finale came when one young girl stood up in class and screamed with venom at him, "We hate you," and the class cheered, "We hate you, we hate you." He threw down *Colette et ses frères* (he, too, was a French teacher) and ran from the room sobbing, his right arm flung across his face. We all snickered. Ten minutes later the short stocky principal came into the room, told us to get in our seats, open our books, and shape up. We moved like bullets. He monitored the hall near our classroom doorway, and we were straight backed, sharp as pencils. The next day a tough substitute teacher came to replace Mr. Moscowitz and we conjugated *to walk, to have, to go, to be* until our young souls were lost in oblivion.

The day Mr. Moscowitz ran out the door was in January. The branches were bare against the gray sky. It was a Long Island winter. Not too bad, not like Chicago or St. Paul. We never saw him again. Twenty-five years later I wonder what happened to him. Where had his life led him? I thank Nancy Vogelsberger for being his only angel. I want to write over and over, "Please forgive us, Mr. Moscowitz. We didn't know what we did." I am ashamed. What I experienced in that class taught me, too, but some lessons take a long time to comprehend.

We are told in art classes that the negative space is important, too. We draw a tree. The blank space around the tree where nothing is drawn has its own integrity, just for the fact that it is there and allows the tree to be there. Mr. Sweeney was my tenth-grade world literature teacher. He acted as the blank space. He counterbalanced the alive energy of his students as they poured into the classroom at the sixth-period bell. He never budged from his big gray desk—pudgy face, black-rimmed eyeglasses, no smile, no frown. He was "placid," a nice word for indifferent. We coexisted in the classroom. He left us alone; we left him alone. We had a list of thirty short stories to read: Katherine Anne Porter, Thomas Mann, James Joyce. We picked up our thick textbooks at a table by the door each day as we entered the classroom, and we read to ourselves. If we finished one story, we went on to the next.

Oddly enough, we did not rebel in this class. There was

nothing to rebel against. Mr. Sweeney put up no opposition. There were no discussions, no papers, no tests. This might sound modern, even avant-garde. It wasn't. Mr. Sweeney was a completely lazy man. I don't remember him reading at his desk, grading papers, or even ever looking at us. He just sat there for the entire semester, like a middle-aged mannikin. Though the authors we read were good choices, our sixteen-year-old minds had trouble understanding those short stories without the help of a teacher. But it was nice for an hour in the school day just to be left alone and I remember that.

Richard Brautigan wrote:

My teachers could easily have ridden with Jesse James
for all the time they stole from me.

(from "The Memoirs of Jesse James,"
in *Rommel Drives on Deep Into Egypt*, Delacorte Press, 1970)

I am delighted whenever I think of that poem. I like the idea of Mr. Sweeney finally getting out from behind his desk, hitching up his gray wool trousers, throwing his leg over a wild pinto pony, and galloping off over the next hill after the next round of helpless students.

Often I have asked friends, "Tell me about a teacher—any grade—who was important to you." They are delighted by the question and then slowly as they think about it, it dawns on some of them, "Why, Natalie, I don't think I ever had a great teacher, someone who really inspired me." If they do think of one, their faces light up. It is a great gift to have a good teacher.

I asked this question of my friend Kate. I can't remember

where we were—the New Riverside Café, Café Latte, someplace in Calhoun Square?—though I am certain that it was in the Twin Cities. I was visiting from New Mexico. Actually, the New French is a good guess, we go there for brunch whenever I'm in town. This question of a good teacher intrigued her. She paused and looked into space for a moment. Then she turned back to me. "You know, Nat, I had Anne Sexton and John Cheever at BU in graduate school. They weren't great teachers in the usual sense; I mean, they didn't teach much, but they were working writers. We had the experience of being with real working writers. Anne Sexton was wired. She would light a second cigarette even while one was in her mouth. At the beginning of the semester, she stood in front of the class and said, 'Now don't you graduate students try to impress me with all you know, I probably haven't read any of it,' and here she had won the Pulitzer Prize." Kate paused. We both had big grins on our faces. "And Cheever. Students brought in their writing and we went over it. He hardly ever said a word. The students commented endlessly. We were all looking to him to say something. When we were done, he had a stock comment for each of us. For instance there was a Hawaiian woman from a Japanese background in the class. He'd say about her work, 'Very inscrutable.' I was a poet, so he'd say, 'Very poetic.' We always complained among ourselves. 'He should criticize us more.' I remember once a student brought in a truly terrible story. We all were snoozing as he read it aloud. There was silence when he was finished. No one had anything to say. Then finally someone plunged in to start criticizing. Cheever just yelled, 'No, stop!' and held up his hand. 'This is the most boring story I have ever heard in my entire life. We are not going to examine it.' The student got defensive, 'Well, it's about the ennui of our society.' 'Yes,' Cheever said, 'the subject can be boredom, but the story can't be boring!' "

Later Kate said to me on the phone long distance— she was working on a new novel, *The Summer of Men*— "About Cheever, it's fifteen years later and I'm getting something now that he said then. I don't know if it makes sense but I was working on my book last week and it bloomed in me. He said, 'Take three disparate objects, you know, like a window, a door, and a can opener, and put them together in a story.' I suddenly really saw what he was talking about. Everyone wants a piece of a teacher, but you don't get that piece till years later."

Often I am asked, who taught me how to write? Everything, I want to say. Everything taught me, everything became my teacher, though at the time I was not aware of all the tender shoots that helped me along, that came up in Mr. Clemente's class, in Mr. Cates's, with all the teachers I can't remember anymore, with all the blank times, the daydreaming, the boredom, the American legacy of loneliness and alienation, my Jewish background, the sky, the desk, a pen, the pavement, small towns I've driven through. The list could go on and on until I named every moment I was alive. All of it in mysterious and ordinary ways fed me. Writing became the tool I used to digest my life and to understand, finally, the grace, the gratitude I could feel, not because everything was hunky-dory, but because we can use everything we are. Actually we have no choice. We can't use what someone else had—a great teacher, a terrific childhood. That is outside ourselves. And we can't avoid an inch of our own experience; if we do it causes a blur, a bleep, a puffy unreality. Our job is to wake up to everything, because if we slow down enough, we see we are everything.

Last December, when I taught a writing workshop in California, I talked about particular authors' lives and their work. I'm thinking of two of my favorites right now: Richard Hugo and Raymond Carver. I discovered Hugo one cold evening in Owatonna, Minnesota. I was down there for a week teaching in the poet-in-the-schools program. I had brought with me a thin volume of his poems, *What Thou Lovest Well Remains American.* I sat in the orange plastic chair in motel room 208 next to the window overlooking the Sears parking lot where snow covered everything, the parking meters and the curbs. I read one of his poems, then stared out at the flurries lit by the street light. Farther down the block was a magnificent bank built by Louis Sullivan. He called it a color-form poem and it was a tribute to America. Inside was a mural of cows and pastel stained glass. I had discovered it the night before. I had stood in front of it, my down hood tight around my face—it was freezing out— and stared up at this building that stood like a god against the dark cold sky. I was amazed that it existed here in this bleak landscape.

I read Hugo on a Tuesday evening in Owatonna after my second day spent teaching verse in an elementary school a mile away. Dark and Jewish, I looked out at a classroom of blond third graders, like a field of sunflowers. One student raised her hand, "Are you Puerto Rican?"

"No," I said.

Italian? Spanish? they guessed.

"No, I'm a Jew," I told them.

They put their hands over their mouths. I had said a dirty word.

Richard Hugo wrote about small towns, not in the Midwest, but in the West—Montana, Idaho. I was primed for reading him in Owatonna. He gave me an entry into the small-town world.

I told my writing group in California that Hugo worked in the Boeing plant in Seattle for eleven years, that he was raised by his aging grandparents, that he played a lot of baseball and was an alcoholic who eventually stopped drinking. He had humble roots; no one seeing his background would have thought he would become a poet.

Later in the week I talked about Raymond Carver. I read from *A New Path to the Waterfall*, poems that he wrote as he was dying of cancer. He, too, had been an alcoholic, divorced after an unhappy marriage. In the last eleven years of his life he was sober and prolific. In the introduction to his book, Tess Gallagher, his partner of those last eleven years, wrote, "Ray knew he had been graced and blessed and that his writing had enabled him to reach far beyond the often mean circumstances from which he and those he wrote about had come, and also that through his writing those working-class lives had become a part of literature. On a piece of scrap paper near his typewriter he had written: 'Forgive me if I'm thrilled with the idea, but just now I thought that every poem I write ought to be called "Happiness." ' "

My voice broke when I read this in class, as it did when I read aloud from Hugo. These writers were my friends and my teachers. They were farther along on the path. They guided me. I had never met either of them, but I loved them through their work. I explained to the class that often when you take on the

voice of a great writer, speak his or her words aloud, you are taking on the voice of inspiration, you are breathing their breath at
the moment of their heightened feelings, that what all writers
ultimately do is pass on their breath. "That is why," I explained
to the class, "you felt in me as I read—and it spread out like
a rain to all of you in the room—that feeling of sorrow, gratitude,
and acceptance. Because that was in these authors' work."

What I didn't realize until later was that in seeking out
these authors, I was also looking for a salve for my personal
grief. I identified with their lives, not because they were women
or Jewish (they weren't), but because they had wrestled through
lonesome, alienated, ordinary beginnings and managed to find
a way through writing to make their lives glow. They had found
a holiness in the center that carried them to satisfaction. I needed
these people, because I came from different but similar American
beginnings. Loneliness and alienation were my dead center inheritance. Though I did not come from the Midwest or from a
small town, I could identify with the doomed lethargy I felt
there, and that lethargy, too, became my education. I learned
from the emptiness, the disconnection with the present, that I
felt all around me. I became that empty myself.

A two-lane highway, a gray day in November, tree branches
bare of leaves scratching a dark sky, one terrible café on the
roadside, just opened in the morning, serving greasy fried eggs
and home fries, the counter strewn with the local paper, buying
a Hershey bar before eight A.M.—that kind of landscape mirrored what I knew of as home. My external family life was
different—my childhood was filled with shopping malls, pot
roasts, housing developments, and three big TVs always on, no

matter what was showing—but it created the same desolation inside me.

My family were pioneers, among the first to move out from Brooklyn to savage nature, to Long Island. From Levittown, we moved even farther out when I was six, about to enter first grade, to that green split-level in Farmingdale, practically the jungle. They were still paving the roads of the development as we rolled up in our blue Buick, my grandparents close behind in their green Plymouth station wagon. The land behind our house was undeveloped. That first year I discovered "my" oak tree and climbed it, found a cave, roamed through a trail of wild berries. The next year they built a GM plant in "my" woods, right in back of our house, and I don't remember even one whimper of a complaint from my parents. After all, wasn't this progress? The plant was lit brightly for the evening shift. I remember going down into the kitchen in the middle of the night to get a glass of cold water from the refrigerator, the GM lights falling in a large square pattern through our bay window onto the green linoleum.

My family read *Newsday*, but there were no books in my home. In my middle teens my father bought a hi-fi and we put it in the cocoa-carpeted sunken living room. We sat on the couch opposite the wooden console and were honestly stumped at what to play on it. Then my father had an inspiration: He ran out and bought a Montovani record. My mother, my sister, and my grandparents approved when they heard it, and we played that one record over and over, nothing else for the first year. Then my father's brother died, Uncle Sam, who lived in a rent-controlled flat on the lower East Side, kept his money stuffed in a mattress, and carried it around with him in a brown paper bag when he went out. He was also a classical music aficionado, and we inherited his record collection. Suddenly we had a pile of Tchaikovsky, Berlioz, and Mozart next to the stereo. My family was curious about these records, and one day we tried Bizet's *Carmen* on the turntable. We frowned: It was too loud, too excitable. We put on Montovani, something familiar, and relaxed again on the couch.

My desolation was that no one knew me and I did not know myself. My family's life was my life. I knew nothing else. I was clothed, fed, given a bed to sleep in, encouraged to marry early and rich, and loved in a generic way—I was "the big one," which meant the older and my sister was "the little one"—but no one spoke to me, no one explained anything.

In all fairness I think my family was stunned to be alive in the twentieth century, eating white bread, buying new products, removed from a community or religious context. Even now when I see my parents, who are in their seventies, they seem a little dazed that they "may" die someday, that they are in Florida far from their children, and that their children are so different from them.

Once when I was visiting my parents, my father and I sat up late one night to watch a movie. The end came earlier than we expected. My father turned to me. "That's just what it's like. You're in your life and suddenly it goes blank. They flash 'The End' across your face."

Everyone in my family was busy, but busy doing what? My mother was busy being on a diet. She ate thin, dried white toast, which she cut diagonally, leaving a line of brown crumbs on the white paper napkin. Then she spread lo-cal cottage cheese over it and drank black coffee. She bought things with credit cards in department stores and then returned them. My father

was busy running a bar, the Aero Tavern, in downtown Farmingdale, going to the race track, eating T-bone steaks with
lots of ketchup, and a wedge of iceberg lettuce with ranch-style
dressing from the bottle. My grandfather mowed the lawn with
the new power mower that automatically collected the cut grass
in an attached pouch. He read the Yiddish paper, smoked stogies,
and sat in a brown suit on a lawn chair in our driveway. Grandma
told me stories and baked cookies. My sister, I suppose, was
lost in her own activities of being the youngest. I never really
got to know her, though we had slept side-by-side in the same
bedroom all our lives.

This alienation is the American disease. It is our inheritance,
our roots. It can be our teacher. Mother Teresa, who works
with India's poorest of the poor, has said that America has a
worse poverty than India's, and it's called loneliness. Mr. Cates
once asked us in class after we read *King Lear*—after Gloucester
plucked out his eyes and Lear anguished over the betrayal by
his daughters—"Which would you prefer? Physical torment, or
mental and emotional suffering?" When we thought about it
enough, no one in class could honestly choose.

Tibetan Buddhists say that a person should never get rid
of their negative energy, that negative energy transformed is the
energy of enlightenment, and that the only difference between
neurosis and wisdom is struggle. If we stop struggling and open
up and accept what is, that neurotic energy naturally arises as
wisdom, naturally informs us and becomes our teacher. If this
is true, why do we struggle so much? We struggle because we're
afraid to die, we're afraid to see that we are impermanent, that
nothing exists forever. My childhood suburbs gave the impres-
sion that they would exist forever, placid, plastic, timeless, and
monotonous, but natural wisdom, the other side of neurosis,
embodies the truth of transiency.

I will give you an example of this transformation of energy from my recent life. Kate, my dear friend, and her three sons, Raphael, age ten, Elliot, age eight, and Jordan, age three, were subletting a house for a month last summer in Taos. Of course, I was delighted; and though I do not have children of my own, I tried hard to include them in activities and not to continually suggest, "Hey, Kate, why don't you get a baby sitter, so we can . . . " I found a brochure advertising an all-day train ride on the old Cumbres and Toltec railroad. I suggested all five of us go on a Sunday. We left Taos by car at seven-thirty A.M. for Antonito, an hour and a half away. I had miscalculated somehow and we arrived an hour early for the train's departure. Kate suggested we have breakfast at the café that was especially for tourists. I said okay—I wanted to be a good sport—and sat among souvenir conductor caps, postcards, flags, and maps, eating white-flour pancakes with fake maple syrup. For the last two months, I had been trying earnestly to cut out all sugar and to eat well. As I poured the artificial maple sugar over my pancakes, I thought, Oh, well, this is a special day. You have to learn to be flexible: You're with kids.

When we settled into our seats on the train, I looked around. Everyone seemed to be from someplace else—Iowa, Kansas, Texas. I shrugged. I don't know why I thought the train should be full of my Taos friends. A man in front of me wore a baseball cap from Texas Instruments; a man behind me had on a GM tee-shirt. These people are on their two-week vacations, I thought. In our small car, I was surprised to see five women with bleached blond hair. They're still doing that? Way back in my high school days, I had known girls who had done that. I felt like a foreigner, in the middle of America.

The train chugged along. It went surprisingly slowly. Uh-oh. This was going to be a long eight-hour ride. As soon as the train began to move, people bolted out of their seats to go to the open-air car in back and to the food car. Kate and the kids went with them. I sat almost alone for half an hour.

After a while I, too, wandered back to the last car. Kate's kids were sucking Tootsie Pops, leaning against a rail, and feeling the wind in their faces. We traveled through empty land full of sage for mile after mile. People were wildly snapping pictures. I wondered what they saw out there. Then I remembered this land was new to them. They asked other people to snap pictures of them standing with their families. Kate offered to take a picture of one family: a husband in a yellow nylon shirt, a wife wearing turquoise earrings, and, in front of them, a son entering adolescence with a rash of pimples across his forehead and a younger boy, clear faced, blond, more innocent, less disturbed. The mother's arm was around the younger boy. The father's arm was around his wife.

"Smile," said Kate. History was made in New Mexico for this Oklahoma family.

I turned to Raphael. "Have anymore of those Tootsie Pops?" I didn't want to be left out. These people seemed to be content. Maybe I could learn to be happy like them.

He eagerly offered to get me one. "What flavor? I have cherry." He held his out. "El has grape." He pointed at Elliot.

"Cherry," I said.

He ran off to the concession stand.

Kate returned with Jordan. She'd just bought him a gray-and white-striped conductor's cap. He did look cute, with a brown curl sticking out the back.

By four in the afternoon, I'd eaten three Tootsie Pops and many Chips Ahoy. We traveled in the dazed rhythm of the train. Elliot had fallen asleep in my lap. All day a strong fear of American "normalcy" had chewed at the edge of my psyche, but I'd successfully kept it at bay, surprised at how I was quietly enjoying myself.

Then, suddenly, a terrible blues descended on me. An old desperation that probably began on nothing-happening Sundays in suburban America when I was a kid. Sunday, the Christian day of rest, was when my friends went to church. We were Jews. We didn't go to church, and in the fifties, the stores and malls that served to fill up suburban life and give the illusion of activity and accomplishment—"I finally found that blue sweater I was looking for"—were closed all day on Sunday. What was left for me, a Jewish kid in Farmingdale, Long Island? No spirit, no religion, a desert of empty shopping centers.

The feeling on the train was familiar: There was nothing for me. My life was bland, and would always be this way, and juxtaposed to this was the nagging feeling that everyone else was having fun, everyone else belonged. They were content, somehow filled up in an America that left me empty.

The feeling descended and I was about to grasp it, hold it hard, and be unhappy, all the while struggling against it. Instead, like an act of grace, I let that old Sunday feeling fall all around me and I didn't grab it. It kept falling and the space opened up—big space, the space I used to be scared of, that told me I was nothing, that made me clutch at my life. Now, yes, it was true I was nothing, but not separate, not alone. I didn't struggle, so I merged with everything around me: kids, Tootsie Pops, the sage, couples in tee-shirts and Reeboks. My life felt empty and jolly and open. Nothing could stop me, freeze me.

I was excited. I had physically experienced what the Tibetans talked about, the transformation from neurosis to wisdom. I sat in the train and watched my letting go, my opening into an old painful feeling, and I experienced it in a new way, felt another dimension of it—its largeness.

I graduated from high school and planned to go away to college. My family never discussed my imminent departure. I simply filled out applications to universities and was accepted at one. I did this all on my own. No one in my immediate family had gone to college and I knew they could not help me.

The end of August arrived. We loaded up my parents' brown Buick convertible and off we went to Washington, D.C. I'd never been there before. I was amazed when we arrived. There were big parks and white buildings, but no skyscrapers. Unlike in Manhattan, I didn't have to bend my head all the way back to see the sky between tall rows of apartment houses. My parents helped me carry my suitcases into Thurston Hall and then up the elevator to the eighth floor. One of my roommates—there were four per room—was already there. She was from Shaker Heights, near Cleveland. We all said hello to her, then my parents and I went back down in the elevator and stood looking at each other in the dormitory lobby. What else was there to do? They had delivered me to college. We hugged good-bye and they walked out the door. I stood there. My mother told me years later that she cried, back in the car. "We just left her. We should have taken her out for juice." I was all alone. My childhood in Farmingdale was over.

But I couldn't get away from home so easily. I studied Plato, Descartes, John Milton, William Blake, Shakespeare. All of it was far away from my roots. It all seemed exciting for a while. I had done it: I had broken out. But I wandered around at George Washington University in a daze. Half of me was still in Farmingdale: I wore clothes my mother had picked out back on Long Island; I dated boys my mother would like. There was no one like Mr. Clemente or Mr. Cates at the school to make what I read alive in my present life. I didn't have a way to digest the new influences of college.

I went to the symphony because my new friends from Boston and Philadelphia went, but I didn't know how to listen to the music. In the audience I mostly daydreamed and curled the program sheet in my lap; then suddenly the music would be over and we would be clapping. One roommate's family had a cook; the girl down the hall had a mother who worked as a scientist. She also swam laps every day. I had never heard of a mother doing that. I tried Mexican food; I tried coq au vin. I made a friend from Georgia and she cooked honey-fried chicken, the way they made it in the South. I called my family every week on the phone, each one taking a turn to speak with me. My sister bought two tickets for a Richie Havens concert, she told me, for when I came home to visit. And my parents told me long distance that they were afraid for us to go to the concert, because of blacks rioting around the country.

Ultimately, all this new college atmosphere wasn't enough to yank me from my roots. I carried my life in Farmingdale within me wherever I went. Personal power could not come from college or an English lit book. It had to come from deep within me. I had to go back and reclaim, transform, what I had inherited at home. Eventually I had to stop running from what I had been given. If I opened to it, loneliness could become singleness; lethargy and boredom would transform into open space. Those fearful, negative feelings could become my teacher. I did not understand this consciously at the time I was in college. I did not know about Tibetan Buddhism then nor what I experienced on that train ride with Kate and her kids so many years later. But if I wanted to survive—no, not just to survive, I wanted glory, I wanted to learn how to grow a rose out of a cement parking lot—I had to digest the blandness and desolation of my childhood and make them mine. I couldn't run away, even though I tried, because in fact, my roots were all I had. If I didn't transform that energy, no matter where I went—Washington, D.C., Ann Arbor, Chicago, California, New Mexico—I would still carry it with me. I would walk around like a numb ghost—and for many years I did walk around numb. Writing became my vehicle for transformation, a way to travel out of that nowhere land. And because writing is no fool, it brought me right back in. There was no place else to go, but moving my hand across the page gave me a way to eat my landscape, rather than be eaten by it.

Actually, the suburbs were ideal for developing a life of cloistered aloneness, a monk's or a writer's life. The childhood emptiness that lurked just under the wall-to-wall carpeting in our living room haunted me. I had to face it sometime in order to become whole. So I kept going back to emptiness: empty roads in Kansas, empty cafés in Minnesota, the emptiness just as August was about to flush its summer grandeur down the long throat of autumn and what I once loved—roses, purple alfalfa flowers, peaches—were gone again for another interminable amount of time. I kept diving into the material of my childhood, and instead of drowning in it, I found a life saver: swimming with my pen.

The deepest thing writing taught me was that there was nothing to hold on to. Thoughts moved quickly. As a writer, I worked hard to grasp them as they flooded through me, but thoughts moved faster than my hand. And thoughts changed. I made up reality as I went along. Nothing was frozen. I wrote about my past, yet there was no place to find it but within myself. It had dissolved out there in Farmingdale where I remembered it.

I discovered this same experience in a poem by Pablo Neruda:

Inside myself I should find the absent ones,
that smell from the lumberyard;
perhaps the wheat that rippled on the slopes
still goes on growing, but only within me,
and it's in myself I must travel to find that woman
the rain bore off, and there is no other way.
Nothing can last in any other way.

("The Wanderer Returned," in
Fully Empowered, The Noonday Press, 1967)

When I became a writer and wrote my first furtive poem at twenty-four years old, I was free. Suddenly the cramped quarters in our split level at 50 Miller Road became big, an arena to explore, and I did not have to wrestle with the ghosts of anyone else's desires. No one in my family had ever dreamed of being a writer. This turned out to be a great gift. I've seen writing students struggle with their parents' unfulfilled writing ambitions and seen how they carry the burden of their parents on their backs. I had none of this. For me, writing was just physically tough; pushing that pen across the page was like pushing my body through a frozen snow field, waist high, in order to get to the other side. I didn't have to live up to anyone else's projected expectations. Writing was totally new, hard, tremendous, and it stunned my family.

When I became a poet, an unlikely thing in my family, almost a useless thing in American society, my parents were enthusiastic, though I made no money at it. I couldn't quite understand it, though I was glad. What I realized later was that deep in our Jewish religion and culture was a reverence for psalms, poetry, songs, the written word, and this reverence echoed out through the years when my parents' daughter began to write. They were happy, with no strings attached. In fact, I think the whole extended family felt a bit of wonder. They especially wanted me to write about them and suddenly exploded with family stories at the dinner table when I visited.

"You know, when I was a boy," my uncle Manny began.

"You were a boy?" I echoed back.

"Yes, there were fields in Brooklyn behind our house and horses grazing," he continued.

"Horses and fields? In Brooklyn?" I said, amazed.

"Yes." He nodded, pleased he'd gotten my attention. Maybe he'd be in my next story.

But it usually happened that a memory ricocheted in my brain back to *me, my* childhood, *my* life. I was a young writer, claiming *me, mine, myself.*

Plato says that the poet takes a momentary leap from ignorance to knowledge and writes a great poem, but because that insight is not built on a foundation, the poet falls back to ignorance again. The poet himself cannot maintain the height the poem achieved. But, Plato says, the philosopher, because he works slowly at his understanding, builds a foundation, so when he arrives at an epiphany he stays there. There is a structure that holds him up. This is the value of practice, done under all circumstances, epiphany or no epiphany; if an epiphany does come, the philosopher is not tossed away, does not fall down afterward.

Writing was the way I learned about practice. I loved writing enough to be willing to work at it, whatever emotional space I was in. Something became more important than my individual mood. Practice sustained me, rooted me. It gave me an unwavering foundation.

My writing practice had probably been germinating all my life with everything in me and outside of me. This is important to understand. Real, solid growth and education are slow. Look at a tree. We don't put a seed in the ground and then stick our fingers in the earth and yank up an oak. Everything has its time and is nourished and fed with the rhythms of the sun and moon, the seasons. We are no different, no more special, no less important. We belong on the earth. We grow in the same way as a rock, a snail, a porpoise, or a blade of grass. America has forgotten this. We are full of aggression, speed. We are full of cancer cells, sped up growth. How many people can we kill with one bomb, how fast can we get a hamburger at McDonald's?

About ten years ago, an elementary school teacher in Minneapolis showed me how a student on a computer could learn to write a haiku. The computer said a haiku was a Japanese poetry form of three lines. It wrote on the screen, "For your first line, pick a season and type it in." I picked "spring" and typed it in. The teacher stood behind me, nodding approval. "You have written the first line of your haiku. Next type in something concrete about spring; for example, 'The birds chirp.'" I typed in, "The willows are green."

"Now pick an emotion and express it." I typed in, "I am sad." It appeared on the screen: I am sad.

"You have finished your haiku," the computer said. Then, quickly, the whole genius haiku appeared in front of the enthusiastic teacher and me:

Spring.
The willows are green.
I am sad.

Then the computer said, "Very good. You have just written
your first haiku. Let's try another one. Usually, a haiku has
seventeen syllables. . . ."

"Isn't this marvelous," the teacher said.

I grinned and stepped away from the machine.

Actually, the haiku I wrote wasn't awful. I've heard worse,
but it had no human element. It had nothing to do with me.
The real essence of a haiku is the poet's awakening, and the
haiku gives you a small taste of that, like a ripe red berry on
the tip of your tongue. Your mind actually experiences a marvelous leap when you hear a haiku, and in the space of that
leap you feel awe. Ahh, you say. You get it. The poet transmits
her awakening.

There are no quick prescriptions for writing. Writing became mine because I wanted it. I lifted my sleepy head off the
desk in public school, smelled Mr. Clemente's rain out the
window, and a seed began to germinate. Something was real
and I could touch it, but that rain happened when I was in
ninth grade. Look how long it took for me to write my first
poem: I was twenty-four years old. I am glad for this slowness.
Out of the lethargy, loneliness, and emptiness of suburbia, if I
slowed down and noticed, my own teacher, the person within
me, had space to emerge. Out of being so lost, the field for
practice came forward. I already knew well enough about rep-
etition—block after block of split-levels with wrought-iron ban-
isters and the home buyer's appealing feature, a sunken living
room. A sunken living room? What, was there a flood?

I had everything. I had to wake up to it. Writing taught

me this. Hours of chewing at a poem made me digest the real personal facts of my life. And there was nothing that wasn't worthy of examination. Suddenly, all of Farmingdale became precious ground. I had a chance to examine slowly what was buried in my psyche back there in my family and childhood.

I wrote about taking the Long Island Railroad with my mother when I was home visiting from my freshman year in college. I was feeling bloated with my new sophistication and despairing at the naiveté of my mother, the housewife. We went to the Museum of Modern Art. I would show her the Impressionists. I'd just learned about them in Art Appreciation I. After all, I'd gotten an A on the midterm. My mother and I stood before Monet's huge painting of water lilies. It was beautiful, more beautiful than the slide my professor showed in class. My mother, who knew nothing of the history of Impressionism, suddenly turned to me. Her eyes were so alive, so magnetic, so black and dancing, she said to me, "Ohhh, Natli, I like this one," and she took my hand. Her eyes frightened me. She had stepped out of the role of beleaguered wife and mother. I couldn't rise to her vulnerability in that moment. I looked away and scoffed, "Wait until you see the Picassos."

I wrote about one day in Mr. DiFrancisco's ninth-grade American history class. It was during the civil rights movement. He read to us aloud from a newspaper article. Somewhere in the South, the Ku Klux Klan had abducted a black man in his twenties. They tied him up on a deserted back road. Then— and here Mr. DiFrancisco choked up. He said, "I can't read this to you kids." We pleaded with him. "Okay," he said, "they cut off his scrotum and plopped it in a paper cup."

Everything stopped for me in that moment. They what? I gulped. I wasn't sure if a penis and a scrotum were the same thing, but I knew something terrible, something violent, had been done. And a male's sexual organ had been mentioned in class.

I took these things to writing practice, tried to make sense of what I carried inside me. Finally, I had a place to express what haunted me.

After I graduated from college, I moved near my boyfriend. He was in graduate school at the University of Michigan. I rented a room from a divorced woman with her three kids, on the second floor of a big rambling house in Ann Arbor, and I sat in the middle of the bed in that room and tried to write. It was different than anything I had experienced before. I was all alone, not lonely. I sat there struggling with my own mind. I put a line down. I crossed it out. I went to the bathroom. I came back, began again, and got excited, couldn't contain that energy, wanted to get up and pace the room. I coached myself. "Stay with it, Nat. Stay with it." I made a deeper furrow into my mind. I began concentrating. Time disappeared. I disappeared. I worked on a poem about chocolate. I invoked Ebinger's Bakery on Church Avenue in Brooklyn, their blackout cake: It transformed into a dark god. It held my entire childhood. I smelled the baking, the garbage in the streets, heard the cash register ring, felt the newsboy on the corner, saw the green container they used to box the cake. This was all coming up from someplace within me. I wrote my first real poem. I had never felt this way before. I looked up. The whole Saturday morning had passed. The shadows of the elms outside my window had shifted to the other side of the yard. This aloneness was good. I was a solitary human being, whole unto myself. This was sacred. It felt *so good*.

. . .

I wanted it bad. I wanted to be a writer. Only in retrospect do I see how badly I wanted it. At the time I wouldn't dare admit that to myself—it was too scary; I felt too insecure, unsure. It takes great power to say, "I want that," and great clarity. My desire took a form more like, "Gee, I like those poets I read in college, Gerard Manley Hopkins, John Milton, W. B. Yeats." I don't even think I thought of them as male. They were writers, that's all. I didn't know that the fact that they were from another century, another country, another gender, and that they were all we read, limited my vision, my confidence, my desire. I wasn't so much intimidated by these male writers as I was unconsciously accepting a structure: Men wrote, women didn't. It was like someone telling you you can't walk in snow. You believe them and then one day you put on your rubber boots and go out and pretty soon you have crossed a large field. What opened up the writing world to me was feminism. Women could write! They could walk in snow. You're kidding! They can? Why I'm a woman! I'll do it. I never thought there was a rule that women couldn't; there was just no perception that they could, no vision of possibility.

When I read Erica Jong's thin volume of poetry, *Fruits and Vegetables,* in Ann Arbor, Michigan, in 1972 at twenty-four years old, I want to say the world exploded. It didn't though. I read about sautéing an onion, cutting an eggplant, and a quiet gully opened between the divided rivers in my brain. One river lived my life; the other knew what to do with that life, having a direction, a consciousness. The gully let the waters come together: A connection was made. Erica Jong was writing about *my* world. At the time I owned a natural foods restaurant called Naked Lunch with three friends. I often spent whole days sautéing onions and cutting up eggplants for ratatouille. I could write about what I lived. I could make conscious, valuable, even deep, my daily life: my walks around the block, my knees, my purchase of toothpaste, the pigeons I saw every morning on the telephone wire, my teeth, my grandmother, her chicken, her challah, her face, my hands, the men I kissed and didn't kiss then, the gray sky of Michigan, the subways of New York and my knowledge of the Hudson River. I could use the material of my life for writing; I could write about Brooklyn, just as Yeats wrote about Inverness.

I threw out everything I had learned in literature classes in college, except my love for it. I threw out the techniques I had learned that writers used: simile, metaphor, style, character, tone, rhythm. The truth was I never understood them anyway. They weren't in my body; they were something Mr. Crane talked about endlessly in a quiet drone. I guess he was a nice man; my dear college best friend Carol, another literature major, liked him, so I kept signing up with her for his courses. We ate those caramel chocolates called turtles in class, passed them to each other, and I liked that. It was enough for me to come and sit next to Carol with her crooked front tooth.

I daydreamed in all the classes, and as we walked into finals in June I grabbed Carol's arm: "What is satire?" Her mouth fell open. Satire was the subject of the entire semester. I had heard not one word of Mr. Crane's lectures. I remember only the dusty cadence of his voice, my heavy eyelids, the gray windowpanes and scruffy black linoleum-tiled floor. "Marry me," I'd sometimes whisper to myself. I have no idea what I meant by that. I wasn't in love with anyone. It was just a motto my mother must have given me or a secret marriage I wanted with literature.

That twenty-fourth year I wrote tentative poems about

lilacs, time, love, light, and dark. I threw in quotes by Thomas
Wolfe, "Oh, ghost come back to me, not into life, but into
magic where we will never die." I'd write these poems lying
on my side on my bed, my left hand holding up my head, and
read them aloud over and over to myself. I was digesting my
own voice. I coined phrases: "In order to write you must have
confidence in your own experience, that it is rich enough to
write about." I had to believe in my mother, my grilled cheese
sandwich, opening the refrigerator, the way I felt about night
and shoulders and sidewalks. My life began to become a vast
field of significant value. The other phrase I repeated was, "You
must trust your own mind." I became aware that writing was
based on words, that they came out of my mind, and that I had
to trust what I thought, felt, and saw. I could not be afraid that
I was insignificant, or stupid—or, I could be afraid, but I had
to speak anyway.

I read slowly through *The Second Sex* by Simone de Beauvoir.
Out of that thick, dense book one line remains for me, and that
line was worth the entire reading. "In order to create you have
to be deeply rooted in the society." She said this to show why
white males, rather than women or minorities, were in the
forefront of art. She gave me the key to creative energy in that
line, "To be deeply rooted in the society." To write I had to
have my fist deep in my life—in my pain, my joy, my culture,
my generation. In other words, I had to be alive. I couldn't be
shut away in the kitchen or the bedroom. I couldn't protect
myself from money, or cars, or politics. Writing is the willingness
to see. I had to be willing to look. Coca-Cola was in my poems,
cigarettes, beer, not because I used any of these—at the time
I was a vegetarian discovering health foods—but because they
were in the landscape around me. I didn't want to turn from
anything because of fear or loathing. In other words—and I

didn't know this then, I know it now—I was slowly, slowly nurturing in me a place of quiet detachment, a place where I could look at everything without judgment, without good or bad, just putting it down on the page.

At that time of lively feminism, I read women authors, but I didn't stop reading men. I just read them differently. I read them as a writer: If they wrote well, if they had mastered that art, I wanted to study their minds, get the essence of what it was to write, but now I could also discriminate. I remember reading *A Moveable Feast*, by Hemingway. His portrayal of his wife Hadley was ridiculous. She was two-dimensional; she sounded like a dingbat. All she did was agree with Ernest: "Oh, Tatie, what a lovely idea," she said to whatever he wanted to do. I didn't any longer believe that this was the way a wife should act. I saw Hemingway's limitation as a writer and probably as a man. Before feminism I'd read books written by men and thought the women characters were the way I should be. I wasn't fooled this time, but wow! could he write about walking through the Luxembourg gardens after working on a short story in a café, about how it felt to write, about how his belly was hungry. This is what I took from him and thanked him for. I'm sure he suffered plenty for his attitudes about women, but I got what I wanted. I studied his sentence length, his rhythms: "On hot nights you can go to the Bambilla to sit and drink cider and dance and it is always cool when you stop dancing there in the leafyness of the long plantings of trees where the mist rises from the small river." (*Death in the Afternoon*, Scribners, 1932.) Hemingway was breathing deep, long breaths to carry this sentence.

I was amazed how the man trusted the leaps in his own mind. Where Hemingway talks about the Bambilla, he also talks about the Madrid climate, sleep, Constantinople, the Allied occupation, watching the sun rise, the stockyards burning in Chicago, and the Republican convention in Kansas City in 1928—all in the same paragraph. He did not worry whether everything followed a topic sentence, as I was taught to write in junior high. Old Ernest went wherever his mind took him. And it worked! I wanted that for myself; that was having a fist in my own life.

What I was doing was slowly studying how one writes. I didn't presume anything; I began at zero. I just examined things and kept hunting for essence. I was neutral; I had no ideas. I didn't believe anything until I tasted it.

This wasn't conscious. If something glowed I went toward it. If it taught me how to write, I ate it up. I had to get really dumb. "Dumb" is a negative word in our society. It wasn't for me. I had to allow myself the dumbness of innocence; I had to become curious and not presume anything. I had to be amazed at the sunrise. I had to let it be a wonder each morning. That is the level I had to ground myself down to.

I remember in third grade, learning how to tell time—or rather, Mrs. Schneider trying to teach me. I couldn't get it. I couldn't compute fall and spring and the rotation of the earth into the arms of this paper clock she held up. Twenty-five minutes to an hour and then a quarter past another hour. I just didn't get it and I was earnest and I tried so hard. "Please, Mrs. Schneider, let's try again," I said, and the class moaned, rolled their eyes to the ceiling. The lunch bell had just rung; we heard the other kids shuffling in the hall, the slam of lockers, the smell of cabbage and potatoes wafting up from the cafeteria. Finally, I gave up something deep and unconscious that I wanted to understand and connect with. I simply said, "Okay, okay, the

long hand at six means 'half past,' " and I left it at that. I broke
the connection with my center in order to appease the class
and my teacher. I learned to tell time, but I gave up duration
and the hugeness of the sun and moon. The class applauded
wildly and dashed for the door, grabbing their lunch boxes and
paper bags full of baloney and ham sandwiches. I shuffled off
with the tuna sandwich my mother made for me almost every
day, the tuna oil smashed into the white bread, turning it soggy.

The problem was a lack of imagination. Why couldn't my
mother think of anything else to make: cream cheese with black
olives, avocado and cheese (did avocados even exist back then,
in the fifties?). What I wanted to understand about time needed
a great act of my imagination. No one in class, including the
teacher, was willing to wait for me to make that connection. It
would have taken too much time. My mind moved slowly.

To learn to write I had to go back to that early innocence,
not taking anything for granted. But this time, I had to be the
teacher, too. And unlike my public school teachers I had to be
patient with the student, allow myself to grow slowly, complete,
full of wonder, connected, and experiential.

In developing writing practice—and remember that at the time
I didn't know I was developing anything, I was just trying to
figure out how to write—I looked to the most elemental things:
pen and paper. I knew writers used paper. Computers weren't
around much then, and I wasn't a good typist. What kind of
pen? What kind of paper? I noticed that my mind—when it
didn't freeze from fear of the blank page—moved faster than
my hand. So then I thought, Well, at least I need a fast-writing
pen. Pencils, I discovered, were too slow, although I liked them.
They were old-fashioned. I liked sharpening them. I liked feeling

the texture of the point against paper. And they were inexpensive. Price was important to me, too. I wanted to be able to write no matter how poor I was. I wanted no excuse not to write. I was searching for the democracy of writing. After all, I was an American. Ballpoints were a little draggy. I liked cheap Sheaffer fountain pens in the beginning. You could get refills, but they often leaked. There was no perfect answer in a pen, but I continued my relationship to them and got to know them for their speed, feel, and texture.

And paper? I realized that I wanted cheap paper, and not loose individual pieces. Spiral notebooks suited me fine. For a while, I searched out unlined ones, but they were harder to find. Again, I wanted no excuse, "Well, I couldn't write this week because I filled my last blank notebook and Woolworth's doesn't have any." Well, Nat, then get a lined one, just get to work.

I wanted to keep my writing—all of it—in one notebook at a time, because I was interested in figuring out who I was. I wanted to study my own mind. I wrote down my mind in the notebook and then read it later. It was a way to digest myself, all of myself. In the spiral notebook, my poems were intermixed with my complaints, my disconnected afternoons, my restlessness—with everything I had to say. Certainly, it wasn't all great writing. I knew I had to allow all of it to just be. In most of my school life, my writing wasn't acceptable. This was the cure: to accept all of it, to make my mind and notebook a safe place. To turn over my mind's garbage and see what could bloom without expectation, with acceptance only.

I know that sounds simple, easy. Well, yes, it was simple, but it was never easy. I was actually asking a big thing of myself: to accept my own mind. The more I wrote the more vast I saw a mind could be. A lot of times I felt I was tripping. Writing became the nondrug high. For many of us who experienced psychedelic drugs, they weren't always fun. LSD took us many places, some dark and terrifying. What the drug did was dissolve our barriers and control. Writing did the same thing. I became immense. I saw I was always immense, but with writing, unlike LSD, it took work to get there and the aim wasn't to be immense or high, the aim was to write, to just be in the soup of my own mind with my notebook spread out in front of me and my hand moving that pen.

And I noticed that the mind was plentiful with excuses. "It's too hot. I'm too tired. My house is messy. My stomach hurts. I had a hard day. I'm lonely. I'm not lonely. I'm too happy, too excited, too broke." I started to call it "the mind," rather than "my mind," because I began to notice there was an impersonal quality. My mind wasn't doing anything to me personally; it was just doing its thing. It was restless, dissatisfied, craving, desiring, detesting, bored, indifferent. I began to see that all of these things appeared every time I sat down to write. At the beginning I gave in to them. I'm tired, I thought. I took a nap. I'm hungry, I thought. I went to the refrigerator. I feel dirty. I took a bath. Each day my complaint felt legitimate and each day I did not write. A week, a month passed. I opened the notebook. I closed it. Sometimes I managed a few lines before I quit. Sometimes, if I managed to assert myself for even ten or fifteen minutes and kept my hand moving across the page, my mind seemed to settle down, it even became content, almost like an unruly child who is deeply craving her mother's discipline and is finally taken to task by her mother.

I also saw that mind was impersonal, because I began to

notice the same elements of avoidance, desire, and ignorance alive in my friends. I began to see that we were all subject to the same shiftings and rumblings and dissatisfactions.

The other thing I discovered: If I had a topic to begin with, it was easier to get started. Almost any topic was okay, because once you began, you entered your own mind and your mind had its own paths to travel. You just needed to step out of the way, but a topic was a first footstep or the twist of a doorknob into the entry of yourself. I began to look for topics, made a list of them in the back of my notebook: apples in August, shoes, my grandmother's feet, stairs I climbed, my first sexual experience. When I sat down to write I could grab one of these topics off the list and begin. But in truth, when I gave my mind its own freedom, no matter what topic I began with—nuclear war, prunes, birth control, hamburgers, Kent State, summer allergies—it all led back to my mother, to that life in the green split-level, my father's bar, my grandparents snoring in the next room. This is what I knew, what I loved and hated, the seeds of my passion.

A writer's life is about examination. What is love anyway, and sorrow, and light? I wasn't ready to examine those things for their own sake. I was busy examining myself. How do I get this mind to speak clearly, how do I coordinate it with my hand and pen, who is a writer, how do I become one? I went to authors' readings and as soon as the writer was done reading, I shot up my hand. "How do you write?" I'd ask. "What is your schedule?" Everyone wrote differently and had a different schedule. That was great! It gave me permission to find my own way. It encouraged me to examine myself. Who was I anyway, who was going to write?

For my tenth birthday, my grandmother offered to buy me a dress. My mother took me to May's department store. There were racks and racks of pink nylon party dresses. I chose one with white lace at the short sleeves and hem, a tight pleated nylon yoke as big as a clown's, a pink ribbon for a belt with an artificial blue flower as large as a small tomato pinned, dangling, to the left side of the waist. It was truly ugly. I loved it. I would have to wear many crinolines.

My mother said, "Are you sure you want this?"

Absolutely. I nodded eagerly.

"But it's winter." She hesitated. "You'll be cold. Well, I guess you can wear your yellow cardigan over it."

We purchased it and I ran ahead, bag in hand, to the parking lot.

My birthday fell on a Saturday. I woke early. I walked into my parents' bedroom. My father was watching television.

"I'm ten! I'm ten!" I said. "I'm two numbers now. One and zero." I held up my index and middle finger, indicating two.

"Wait until you have three numbers," my father said.

My mind quickly spanned through the twenties, thirties, forties. I would have to be very old to get to three digits. I was going to be in the two-digit numbers a long time! I might never get to the three. I looked up. My father was joking. I laughed.

We were going to New York City for the day. We would take the Long Island Railroad in Wantagh. I got to invite my best friend, Jo Ann Carosella, who lived next door, to come with us. Her parents had a gray Cadillac with the first automatic windows I'd seen. When her father pulled it up in their driveway for the first time, we all ran over.

"Blow on the window," Richard Carosella, Jo Ann's older brother, demanded. I blew and the window magically went down.

To New York City the five of us went: my parents, me,

Jo Ann and my sister, who was seven. I sat on the train in my pink nylon dress, brown leggings underneath, heavy brown overcoat, white nylon socks, and black patent-leather shoes. It was a cold January day.

We ate lunch at Lindy's on Seventh Avenue. I ate a chopped steak burger and their famous cheesecake that all the Broadway stars ate.

Then, what should we do? My father suggested a matinee. There was a movie theater around the corner. We could go there. Yes, everyone agreed. The marquee said *Peyton Place*. We'd never heard of it, but we were sure it would be good.

We settled in our seats with popcorn and Jujubes, a colored chewy candy, my favorite.

The velvet curtain swung open; the movie began. We were about a quarter of the way into the movie—someone was in love with someone, the popcorn was delicious, I put big gobs into my mouth—when I suddenly felt my parents' nervousness. I looked up. They were casting worried glances at each other across the tops of our heads. They were flanked on either side of the three of us. The girl in the movie, very pretty, with red lipstick, who was in love with the man, was just about to tell him—my father and mother both stood up, jerked us out of our seats, and ran us up the aisle.

"What? What?" I whined, as I was pulled along, my hand in my mother's. "What's happening?" My head was turned around to see the last moments of the screen before we went through the front doors of the theater.

My mother hissed. "She's pregnant. She's going to tell him she's pregnant."

"Pregnant? How could she be pregnant? She's not married," I said.

"Never mind," my mother said, as she dragged me out

into the afternoon sunlight of midtown Manhattan. We stood a little stunned in front of the theater.

My father had an idea: "Let's take the subway to Greenwich Village. We can see the beatniks," he said.

"What are beatniks?" I asked, my head cocked to one side.

"They wear black turtleneck sweaters, smoke cigarettes, and read poetry in front of jazz bands," my father explained.

"What's jazz?" I asked.

"Some terrible, noisy music," my mother chimed in.

"Oh," I nodded.

Instead of taking the subway, we took the Fifth Avenue bus downtown. I looked out the window and saw a man in a brown hat smoking a cigarette, standing on a corner selling pretzels. I wanted one.

"What's that?" I pointed to a woman in a navy overcoat standing over a black pan with something smoking.

"Chestnuts," my mother explained.

We walked around Greenwich Village and weren't sure if we saw beatniks or not. As we walked, my father added another clue.

"They also wear goatees," he said, and showed us with his gloved finger on his own face the shape of a goatee.

We nodded. My little sister was not that interested. She ran open-armed after pigeons in Washington Square, hoping to hold one. They flew ahead of her. Jo Ann's feet were getting blisters from her party shoes. She wanted to sit down on a bench, but I was intent on finding a beatnik. I walked around and stared into men's faces—it never occurred to me, or to my father, that women could be beatniks. I thought I almost found one, but he was wearing a tan overcoat. I couldn't tell if he was wearing a black turtleneck underneath, but he did have a goatee and was carrying a satchel. Maybe it contained a poem. He flicked the last bit of a Camel into a garbage container.

I went back to the bench where my family was and I reported my find.

My sister wailed, "I'm hungry."

It was five o'clock. Time for dinner. We walked down a wide street, looking for a restaurant.

Crepes, a sign hung over our heads.

"Let's go here," my mother said, and before I could ask, she turned to me. "Crepes are French pancakes. We're going to have a French meal."

The maître d' seated us at a table with a red and white checked tablecloth. There were wood shavings on the floor. All the waiters were dressed as cowboys with ten-gallon hats, pointed boots, fringe on their shirts and jeans—we called them dungarees.

I ordered cherry crepes. When the waiter walked away, I asked, "How come they're dressed as cowboys?"

"This is New York," my father explained.

Of course. I nodded.

Just as they served us bread in a basket with small pats of butter in a white dish, the two double front doors swung open and were held. The cold air blew in; we all turned in its direction, and I put my coat over my shoulders. Tourists from a New York City tour bus swarmed in. The bus driver, with a mike, announced, "Ladies and gents, just take a table. We're eating like they do in Gay Paree and Gene Autry and Hopalong will be glad to serve you." I looked at the waiters. Was Roy Rogers here, too?

My mother hated her omelet with cheese and mushrooms. She was particularly disappointed, because this was the day she let herself off her diet.

At the end of the meal, the maître d' returned to our

table, his thin mustache twitching—I wished it was a goatee—under his big cowboy hat.

"And, madam, did you enjoy your meal?" he asked as he bent to take my mother's empty plate.

"Your food stinks," my mother hissed and nodded her head in a final condemnation.

The waiter was taken aback. "But, madam . . . "

My mother turned her head away. It was clear there would be no further discussion. She had made her decree.

My father bent over the bill, mumbling.

I liked my cherry crepe. It was French.

We rode home on the railroad. It was dark as we traveled through Rockville Centre, Baldwin, Merrick, the lights of towns made into white and yellow streaks by the speed of the train.

This was my tenth birthday.

Who was I, anyway, who wanted to write?

PART
TWO

By accident, not intended, not even wanted, I had a deep awakening experience in front of a sixth-grade class I was teaching in the Northwest Valley in Albuquerque, New Mexico.

I was wearing a white button-down blouse, gray slacks. I had my hair pulled back with a barrette. I stood near the third row, the blackboard with a map of the world pulled down was behind me, and I was twenty-six years old. I was an ardent atheist—only "lit-er-a-chure" would save me. I had studied Descartes, Kant, Plato. I believed in reason, rationality. I had been hired in the middle of the school year; the veteran teacher of eleven years had quit because she couldn't control this particular group of Hispanic and Indian kids, and I was next in line to try my fortitude and courage. This was my first time in a contracted teacher's position. I had received my teaching certification six months before, in Ann Arbor, Michigan. I said yes immediately when Mr. Jones, the school district personnel manager, called me. He said the other teacher was taking a leave of absence to pursue a Ph.D. It wasn't true. She told me she was beat, exhausted, and she also told me which kids to watch out for, when I visited the class on her last day of duty. I wasn't even supposed to teach English, the only thing I knew. I was supposed to teach social studies, a subject I knew nothing about, but I tried. I was in New Mexico, naive about the state, its culture and customs.

That morning, three men in suits had appeared at our classroom door. They knocked.

"Yes," I said, "please, class, be still." The class was never still. They did not become still then either, but they were curious. They half sat in their seats.

"We're from Cuba," one of the men said. "We're here to study your school."

"Cuba! Come in. Come in." I ran to the blackboard and stood before the world map.

"Now who can point out Cuba for me?"

Skinny Roberto ran down the aisle between two rows of desks. He pointed his finger to Costa Rica. I adjusted it to Cuba.

"Yes, that's it." I turned to the three men. "How did you pick our school?"

They look bewildered. One said, "Our principal sent us," and they quickly excused themselves.

The lunch bell rang. The kids ran out the door. I went to the teacher next door.

"Mrs. Martinez, you're not going to believe this. There were three men here from Cuba! Can you imagine? They picked our school."

She looked up from her desk. She was about to pop a Chiclet into her mouth.

"Miss Goldberg, they came from Cuba, *New Mexico*. Not Havana, Cuba. Cuba's a small town north of here."

"Oh," I said, and backed out of her class. My face turned red.

I sat down at the steel desk in my classroom, opened a drawer, took out a container and scooped strawberry yogurt into my mouth. I rubbed the chest bone over my heart. It was sore. The night before I had been so busy writing a short story about my grandfather's orange bowl that I forgot two eggs I'd left on the stove to boil. Suddenly I smelled something burning and jerked up from my desk and bolted into the kitchen. As I turned the corner I ran into the refrigerator; the handle hit me hard in the chest. I fell back, staggered, and saw stars. They were the same stars I'd seen the weekend before on a wall painting at the palm reader's.

I had been driving down highway 25 just outside of Albuquerque when I passed a small adobe house with a huge white sign of a red hand with red lettering, Know Your Future. I quickly swung into the driveway. I thought to myself, what are you doing? I don't believe in this.

I knocked at the door. A seventeen-year-old Chicano girl answered. I lied and said I was a student, so I could get the two-dollar discount she told me about. I followed her through a dining room, past a brown velvet couch, a television set, and a black velvet painting of a tiger hanging on a yellow wall, and into a back room separated from the rest of the house by a curtain of beads.

Christ, a wood sculpture of his head, was on the wall, and next to it that painting of gold stars on a blue-black background.

I thought, oh, Jesus, I don't believe in this.

She told me to hold out my hand.

I held it out.

"Um, you're very sure of yourself. Your whole way of seeing and understanding is going to change."

Oh, yeah, I thought. "When's this going to happen?"

"Soon."

"How soon?"

"Very, very soon."

I rolled my eyes. I argued with her. That wasn't going to happen. "Anything else?" I asked.

"You're going to go someplace you've never been before. Where you know no one. Into the deep north. You'll do this for the love of a man." She held my hand.

Oh, brother, I thought. I was a strong feminist. I wasn't going to drop everything for a man. "Yeah, when will this happen?" I asked.

"Not for a long while. In the future."

I had had enough. I pulled my hand away. I put it forward again. I started to ask about writing, I pulled it back again.

I paid her the three dollars and left and forgot about it.

When I ran into the refrigerator handle, I remembered the palm reader, the dusty road, the turquoise sky, the rock cliffs behind her house, and the star painting behind her left shoulder.

Stunned, I turned off the stove. The egg shells were burned brown and the pot was black. There was an awful smell in my apartment. I threw the eggs and pot in the garbage.

My chest still hurt. I had fifteen minutes before the kids returned to the class. There were paper planes on the floor, at least fourteen of them. Paper clips, textbooks, pencils, empty Frito-Lay orange-and-red cellophane bags, a whistle, three sweaters, and two pairs of sneakers also were on the floor. The wooden desks with attached chairs were in jagged rows, some turned all the way around and facing each other.

After I finished my yogurt and dumped the container in the wastebasket, I just sat at my desk and waited for the bell to ring.

When it did, the kids charged into the class in jean jackets and sweatshirts. It was April. They ran to their seats.

I stood up in the middle of "Please, please, be quiet," and suddenly stopped. The place where my chest was sore—it was opening, opening red and enormous like a great peony, and it was radiating throughout my body. I felt the blood flowing in my hands and legs. I turned and looked out the window. I looked at the smoky appearance of the spring cottonwoods near the parking lot. Any day now they would break into leaf. There was a spindly Russian olive near our window. Suddenly it looked beautiful. Then I had one simple vision: I saw myself wandering in autumn fields and I felt that nothing, nothing else was important. This was a profound feeling, a big feeling. It wasn't a passing, momentary flash. I knew I had to stay true to that one vision.

Understand, I had no idea what was happening. It wasn't some glorious enlightenment that many of us imagine and wish for. I was frightened. I didn't want it. I just wanted to be a writer and to earn a living keeping this class in front of me quiet. I didn't understand what was going on, and I had no clue about those autumn fields. Just then, there was a fist fight in the corner between Henry and Anita, the toughest girl in the class, and the spectators were enthusiastic. I had signed a contract, my first. I hated my job; I wasn't qualified for it—which, in this case, meant keeping control of everyone—but that didn't matter. I was going to get through it. I had two months until the end of school and now something was inside me and I had to stop that fight.

When I got home that night I called a friend.

"Gabrielle, my heart opened in front of the class. Nothing makes sense."

"I don't know what you're talking about," she replied. She was an intellectual. She, too, had read Kant, Descartes, Henri Bergson, Aristotle.

I hung up. None of my friends wanted to hear about it. They all were like the person I'd been before this afternoon in class: atheists, intellectuals.

At two in the morning, I bolted up in bed, wide awake. I got up and walked into the living room, sat down on the couch and stared at the kitchen clock over the refrigerator in the other room. My mind was totally blank. I just stared. I didn't go back to sleep until five A.M. I had to wake up for school at seven. I was exhausted the whole next day in class.

This waking up and staring in the middle of the night continued for three weeks. It became clear that I should quit my job and go to the mountains. Simultaneous with this clear feeling was another voice in me: "What! Are you crazy? You've signed a contract. If you quit, you won't get another one. The mountains! You're a city girl. You don't know anything about the mountains!"

The kids continued to run around the classroom. I became quite fond of several of them, and I was tired from no sleep and strung out between my heart and my teacher's contract.

Finally on one Monday in school, without plan or thought, I went next door to Mrs. Martinez and asked her to watch the class. I marched down the just-waxed linoleum corridor lined with tan lockers to the principal's office. I have no idea what I said to him as I sat across from him at his large brown desk, because while my mouth, connected with my body, spoke one thing, my busy mind was screaming at me, "What are you doing? You're crazy. You're finished! You'll starve in a gutter." I must have been eloquent, though, because when I was finished, Mr. Peterson, the principal, stood up, gave me a strong handshake, and said, "I understand completely. And if you ever want a job again, just call me."

I felt such relief. I flew down the hall back to my class. I was free. This was my last week trying to get the kids in their seats. As a matter of fact, when I entered the class again, after thanking Mrs. Martinez for watching them, I thought, "What the hell. Let them do what they want. They do it anyway." I sat behind my desk the rest of the afternoon, smiling. We all seemed happier and, given freedom, they seemed less unruly.

On Tuesday I took attendance and then lined them up at the door. I didn't have a plan but I was sure one would emerge. I marched them outside and along the weedy road. Just being outside made us all happy. We walked for a quarter of a mile and I saw the Staff of Life sign in the distance. I remembered it was a food coop on five acres of land, with swings and paths and an herb garden. We headed toward it, and for the whole morning the kids gathered in small groups, played, and were content. The coop people were thrilled. They were getting a chance to educate the youth. They ran out intermittently with samples of organic carrots and roasted corn. Anita even said she could definitely taste the difference between organic and non-organic carrots and she liked the organic better, said she was going to ask her mom to buy some.

Each day of that week we did something different. I trusted something inside me, instead of what I thought I should do, and the kids responded. Because I was leaving soon, I didn't feel the restraints of the public school. It was as though that institution was no longer between me and the kids, that massive brick structure had crumbled, a new path had opened, a new way to be together. It wasn't all obvious to me at the time, but it was the beginning of something new.

On Thursday it rained. The kids were dismayed. We wouldn't be able to leave the building.

"Nonsense," I said. "It's not cold out and it's not raining hard. Let's get very still." I waited for them to become still and they did, unlike a few weeks ago. "When we go out and enter the rain, see if you can walk between the drops." I paused. "If we do get wet, don't worry—it's New Mexico!" In one enormous rush, I felt the whole glory of the state. "We'll dry quickly."

I led them to the front door. They were excited and a

little nervous. We were breaking a rule: You couldn't get wet
by rain, only by swimming in pools, by sprinklers, showers, and
never in school. I was happy, fearless. I was taking that girl in
Mr. Clemente's class out from behind the desk and into the
downpour.

I stood by the door. "I will demonstrate. All of you watch
and then you can follow." They stood huddled in the entry way.
I stepped out, no raincoat, no umbrella, my palms up and open
in supplication to water. I stepped along the sidewalk.

I went up to a bush, picked a twig, turned to face the
group and said, "Ahhh, sagebrush smells best in the rain. Come
slowly and enter it."

They stepped away from the building like the patients in
the movie *King of Hearts*, who had been freed from the insane
asylum. They stepped out into the rain gingerly, tenderly, and
were delighted.

On Friday, I stood in front of the blackboard. "I have
something to tell you." They were all attentive. "Today is the
last day of the week and the last day I'll be here." There was
an awkward, stunned silence. "Look, I know, this has been a
tough year for you. Let's face it, none of you were dolls. You
weren't that well behaved." Alvaro, Roberto, and Eloy smirked.
"But this week was a great week." They all nodded. "I want
you to remember it. It's important. All of you get in your
seats"—they were leaning against bookshelves and sitting on
top of desks—"and when you do, I want you to close your
eyes and put out your hands." I walked around and placed a
Hershey's Kiss in each kid's palm. "Now unwrap it, and all on
the same count, when I say yes, put it on your tongue, close
your eyes and your mouth, let it melt slowly, and remember
this week. Promise to never forget it, no matter what else
happens in your life." I switched off the classroom lights.

I felt sad and happy when I left that day. I had begun to redeem something from a long time ago, all that deadness I had felt as a child.

A few days later someone told me to check out the Lama Foundation, a commune that had spiritual retreats, seventeen miles north of Taos. It was started by Ram Dass as a place to further consciousness. His book *Be Here Now*, about his experience in India and his recipes for being in the present, was put together there. I had read it years before when I lived in Ann Arbor and was impressed by it, though I didn't understand it then. The Lama Foundation had an open house every Sunday.

I drove north in my Volkswagen Beetle, made a right at a sawmill and drove down a long, circuitous dirt road that took me up Lama Mountain. There were white and faded pink squares of material hanging from trees along the road—prayer flags, I learned later—and then a wooden sign that said: Park: the rest of the way you go on foot. I parked; I followed the dirt path. About halfway up, a woman six feet tall, barefoot, wearing a long white robe, was coming in the opposite direction.

"What are you doing here?" she asked bluntly.

I looked up. I clasped my hands to my breast. "The Garden of Eden opened up in my heart and I don't know what to do," I blurted out, earnestly.

"You must find a practice to water that garden," she said without missing a beat.

I was so grateful. "You mean you understand?"

"Of course I do," she said.

After that day I drove back to Albuquerque, gave notice to my landlord, packed my things and moved up to the Lama Foundation. It felt right. I was trusting something that wasn't logical. I took a leap of faith. I'd never been in a place like Lama before.

. . .

Someone gave me a tipi to live in on Lama Mountain and a
man named Siddiq, who was an exphysicist from Berkeley, taught
me how to meditate—to sit cross-legged, back straight, hands
on knees, and to feel my breath go in and out at my nose. I'd
never paid much attention to my breath before. I had been
breathing since I was born, but now I noticed it. As I sat, my
attention wandered all over the place—to a fly on my knee, to
a memory of my grandfather's hat, to a thought of chocolate—
but my breath continued, physically there throughout the time
I sat, and then, I realized in amazement, throughout my life.
And I discovered breath had different qualities all by itself,
without my controlling it. Sometimes it would be deep, at other
times shallow. It felt like the measure of the line when I wrote
poetry: short lines, staccato breath; long lines, I'm breathing
way down in my belly. I saw, too, that my breath also determined
how much I could write at one time, it made language physical,
it propelled the sentence. Also, breath connected me to my
body. Whether my mind wandered or not, my body stayed in
the cross-legged position. It was here, whether I was or not.

Each week we prepared for a new teacher to come up to
Lama. The second week I was there, Baba Hari Dass visited.
He was an Indian sadhu who hadn't spoken in twenty years.
He'd made a vow never to speak again. It used up prana. Prana
is breath and essential life energy. Baba Hari Dass was a yogi.
He'd lived in the jungle alone for fourteen years, and for those
years he ate only two bananas and a cup of milk a day. Also
he'd never cut his hair and wore it wound up on the top of his
head. He communicated by writing on a blackboard. When I
walked into the dome where he sat on the first day of his visit,
surrounded by his followers, he looked up at me. He was beau-

tiful, with sharp black eyes like drops of fresh-cut coal. I felt
very conspicuous. I wore khaki bermudas, a tee-shirt and short
hair. Many of the people at Lama had been to India, wore white
robes, had long hair—the men included—a ring in their nose,
several in their ears.

Hari Dass wrote on his blackboard, "What do you do?"
and then he turned the board so I could read it.

"I teach English," I said. Even in my awkwardness, I had
this one identity. I cared about language, writing, literature, but
I felt silly saying it.

He smiled and wrote on his board, "Will you teach me?"
Everyone laughed. I felt immediately okay, warm, accepted.
I wasn't weird, odd, out of place. I sat down and joined in the
singing. Here was a teacher who spoke to my whole person. I
felt good, simply good, in his presence.

The following week, Rabbi Zalman Schacter came to teach. We
celebrated a luxurious Sabbath with a big challah we baked that
day, lots of food, dancing, prayers, singing.

On that Monday I received a letter from my mother.
"Please call us immediately," she wrote. There were no phones
at Lama. I had to drive down the mountain that night into
Questa, the nearest town. I found an outdoor pay phone at a
food market and called my parents collect.

"Come home. Your father's having a nervous breakdown
and you're up there in a commune with Charles Manson."

"Mom, I'm not with Charles Manson. As a matter of fact,
a rabbi is up here right now. What's the matter with Daddy?"

My father's older brother had died six months earlier and
hadn't mentioned my father in the will. Though my father didn't
care about being left money, he wanted to be recognized. My

mother told me he would stand at the bar, wiping the countertop with a white cloth and talk to his brother in his mind. "Jacob, I loved you so much. You didn't mention me in the will, like I never existed for you. I didn't care about the money, but at least to say, 'And Buddy, remember I loved you.' Nothing. All that love wasted." And right there in the bar, in the middle of the day, in front of his customers, my father would break down crying.

"Why doesn't he take some time off?" I asked. As I stood by the road, the mountain air grew chilly. I buttoned up my sweater.

"He can't. He has to work. Why don't you come home?" she insisted.

"I don't know. I'll let you know. Send him my love." I hung up. I felt confused. I was happy where I was. I didn't know what I could do for my father.

I pulled out of the parking lot and didn't see a young motorcyclist coming toward me. He curved wide in order to avoid my car and ran into the sage. I stopped. He was okay, but he was screaming at me. "You dumb fuck, look where you're going."

I burst out crying and drove up the mountain sobbing for my father, his brother, for the distance between us. I parked at Lama. The moon was near full. The forest was silver with dark shadows. Just as I got out of my car, Rabbi Zalman walked by.

"Rabbi," I called out. He came over. He could see I had been crying.

"What is it, *mamala*?" he asked, putting his hand to my face.

"My father's having a nervous breakdown. They want me to come home. I think I want to stay here," I blurted out.

"You are doing a beautiful thing being here. You stay here. I will pray for him. Tell me, what is his name, your father?"

"Benjamin."

"And his mother's name?"

"Rose."

"I will pray for Benjamin, the son of Rose. He will be all right. You be happy here."

I smiled. I *was* happy. I did not want to go.

The next day I wrote a long letter to my parents and stayed at Lama. A month later, without my help, my father was back to normal.

All through that summer, I met different religious teachers. An American Indian came to work with us, a Sufi, a Catholic monk. All these teachers were different from the ones I had met in public school and college. They did not make a weekly salary, keep regular daily school work hours, wear suits, teach from books, have us sit at desks. What they taught was their way of life. It did not end at the end of a work day. Their work was integrated with everything they did. And what we learned most from them was who they were as people, and that each one had a path—Judaism, Christianity, Hinduism—to refine who they were.

In algebra class, it didn't matter so much what Mr. Johnson was like as a person. In fact, he was rude and mean, he humiliated Milly Polson for not having a clean cover on her textbook and a sharpened pencil, but we could still learn from him the area of Q divided by the square root of A. Mr. Johnson disseminated information; his job was not to transmit his being.

The teachers up at Lama transmitted who they were, how

they saw the world, how they struggled with their own human lives, and how they understood what it meant to be human in relation to plants, animals, inanimate objects, the earth, and the heavens. They ate with us; they took walks with us; they prayed and sang with us.

This was what I had been dying for through all those empty classroom hours. When Mr. DiFrancisco, my ninth-grade American history teacher, paused from writing dates on the blackboard to tell us he wouldn't be in the next day because he was getting married, the entire class rippled with life. We were thrilled. The man up there writing 1892 on the board was a human being, he must have kissed a girl, and after tomorrow night, he was going to "do it," our reference to intercourse. I couldn't wait for the following Monday to see the ring on his finger—his left hand: I knew that much.

The Lama teachers also gave us a practice, something to do on our own after they left, a way to begin to teach ourselves. Hari Dass taught us yoga and pranayama, breath exercises; Rabbi Zalman shared Sabbath and prayer; a Sufi teacher showed us dancing and swirling and singing. In public school, I generally forgot everything about world history as soon as the school year was over. These teachers taught us something central to the rest of our lives and a way, a practice, to continue it.

Many of these religious teachers still had old ideas about women, but most were also deep enough not to be frozen by their ideas. No female teachers came to Lama while I was there. By that time, I was a staunch feminist, but I was willing to put it aside, or to try to keep quiet about it, because there was something there I wanted badly, and I didn't want to get caught in feminist arguments. I wanted to get as much as I could of what these teachers had. Later I would make it mine, make it woman-centered.

. . .

I liked all the teachers—my heart was open—but I discovered that my real interest was meditation. None of the teachers I met at Lama spoke directly about it, but some of the Lama staff sat in meditation regularly and I sat with them every morning and every evening in the small adobe kiva that was built next to the dome. It was the first thing I did when I woke up in the morning and the last thing I did before I went to sleep. The Lama staff taught me different techniques: to count the breath, to visualize a full lotus on my forehead, to name different sensations in my body. I tried them all a time or two, but in truth, all I wanted to do was sit down, finally, with my own mind, and watch it.

The landscape of the writer is the mind and I was fascinated with it. I saw that I kept thinking, that I couldn't stop. Every time I tried to pull my attention back to my breath, another thought came. Suddenly, it felt obvious: This is what I had wanted to do for a long time, to sit in the raw nakedness of myself, with nothing else but myself. No parents, no culture, no New York background, no workshop, teacher, school. Just who was I? Where did I come from? How was I becoming a writer, given my family? What part of us is born apart from family? How was I heading in a whole different direction from my upbringing, from anyone I knew in Farmingdale, and how was I so alone and different in school? These questions were all unconscious. Mostly, I wanted quiet, for things around me to shut up, so I could finally hear my own mind, settle into it.

I was drawn to essences. And I was a practical person. Meditation was simple; you needed nothing but yourself. You could sit down anywhere and do it. You didn't even need a pen and paper, as you did for writing. It was economical. I watched

how thoughts changed: I remembered my apartment in Albuquerque, then a gardenia my friend had on her chest of drawers.
I let my breath out and I thought of a river I knew in Sandusky
County, Ohio; of how I had recurring thoughts: I was planning
meal after meal in my head—pot roast dinners—then deciding
on vegetarian cuisine; and of how some thoughts I clung to hard
and fed with my anger or sadness or hope: I worried about my
grandmother. By the time I was at Lama, she was in a nursing
home in Long Beach. I thought of her often and longed to have
her near. I was being introduced to my own mind, but now
without even the activity of writing. It was austere, rugged,
huge.

Just recently, when I asked a writing friend of mine why he's
taking so long to write his novel—it's been seven years and
there's no end in sight—he said, "I'm afraid of the quiet when
you sit down alone. It's easier for me to keep busy. I'm stunned
by how quiet it is when I sit down at the desk."

That was a very honest answer, direct, genuine. I understood what he was saying. In a sense, meditation and writing
go hand in hand. The more deeply we can allow ourselves to
sink into the darkness of our own selves, the more we can settle
into the mind of being a writer.

We're all fascinated by writers. I remember hearing that
Tennessee Williams and Carson McCullers were friends. They
rented a house in southern France one summer and each morning
they both sat at the kitchen table and wrote. Wow! I thought,
those two. I imagined them digging into their own imaginations,
and though their bodies were across from each other—I easily
imagined the white cups of steaming half-drunk black coffee,
the only-nibbled-at golden croissants, heavy cream, strawberries,

hunk of Gruyère cheese, long baguette on the table between them—they were both deep into the separate countries of their vast minds. I think the power I felt from them, from any writer whom I imagined, was that they had access to their own inner worlds. They could sit still in one place, concentrate, and words would pour forth. I think this is why so many people in America want to write. It is not because Americans are gaga about literature—oh, if only we were!—it is because we are so disconnected and isolated as individuals and as a country that one way to reconnect is to begin with a connection to ourselves. Writing is a way to connect with our own minds, to discover what we really think, see, and feel, rather than what we think we *should* think, see, and feel. When we write we begin to taste the texture of our own mind. This can often be frightening. We look around. There's no one else there. We come face to face with our own aloneness, sit in our own loneliness. It is hard, painful, but it is real. Americans long for this realness and often don't know how to get to it.

I was up at Lama with all these things in my arms: loneliness, my vast human mind, writing, breath, the Garden of Eden in my heart. A classroom teacher could no longer help me, nor any textbook. In the fall, when it grew too cold to live in my tipi, I moved into the town of Taos, among the tall cottonwoods turning yellow and the smell of juniper and piñon wood smoke. One evening, walking past the Taos Inn, I smelled the smoke clearly in the chilly air and I thought, I would leave everything for that smell and the way it filled the huge space below Taos Mountain. I had a boyfriend then and together we sat meditation and wrote. We lived in a thirty-dollar-a-month adobe with no running water, an outhouse, wood stoves, and dirt floors. In winter, I watched snow fall among the piñons that dotted the hills and I watched how Taos grew silent and deep and I walked often by the Rio Chiquita and down by the Rio Grande. We were among the hippies; we looked like hippies, we were poor like them, but we had entered a path—the path of writing and meditation.

In those years, I had no aim for my writing; I just did it, as I did meditation. The two became coincident for me. I would sit under a tree, lean against a rock near a stream, or be at my kitchen table and keep my hand writing and let my mind churn up whatever it had to. In a sense I was my mind's record keeper. I was examining the texture of my thoughts—how they moved and how they came up.

The hippie years served me well. I had a culture to support my aimlessness, my pennilessness. If the culture you live in has no money and does not value it, it gives you the freedom not to have it, too. I never worried about earning a living or making money. I made enough for food and rent teaching writing part-time at a hippie school. I surmised the worth of practicing the hippie values of aimlessness, being here now, no future, no past, nothing to do, nowhere to go, but I saw how hard it was to really live or achieve that kind of undirected openness: to write for the sake of writing, not for publication, not even to write something good, just to write; to sit and watch my breath, not to become peaceful or enlightened, just to sit, just to breathe, to receive my life. Very simple, very hard. I remember often saying in those years, "I want to learn to do nothing." Perhaps it was a rebellion against our "do something" society, but the nothing, no-thing emptiness I groped for was also something much deeper than rebellion, and I was not sure what it was. The womb of hippie life protected me for my serious exploration of this nothing.

I had no writing teacher. I had no meditation teacher. I stopped reading books, except for an occasional Salinger, *Franny and Zooey, Nine Stories,* Ken Kesey's *One Flew Over the Cuckoo's Nest,* and oddly enough, one night I coaxed some friends into reading aloud with me the play *Our Town,* by Thornton Wilder. I stopped reading books because I wanted to stop referring to an external authority. I read something only if it grew naturally out of what I was doing. For the first time in my life, I wasn't involved with school and books. This was important to me. I was meeting myself without any outside reference. I noticed the wild plums along the ditch, the magpies, the rose hips in fall. The moon had a size and its size changed in the sky and I noticed those changes. It was as though I had a chance at a second childhood. I felt wonder: I looked into the face of a sheep, a horse, a cat. I went camping and backpacking alone. I'd never been in the woods alone before. I made friends with trees, a stream, a chipmunk.

I stepped forward naked to meet the world around me by noticing, looking, feeling, digesting it and I was also meeting the world inside me through meditation. Every moment and everything became my teacher. This was so different from what I had been taught education was. I was hungry, delighted, happy.

A woman named Maggie Kress moved to Taos from California, and bought a beautiful pink adobe near where we lived. I heard she'd been a Zen student, that she had been close to Suzuki Roshi, the Zen master of the San Francisco Zen Center, author of *Zen Mind, Beginner's Mind,* who had died of cancer a few years before. I was curious about her. I went over to visit. My friend Sassafras—lots of people had hippie names then; there were Rainbow, Cement, Snowflake, Running River—was doing some carpentry work for her. I can't remember anything we talked about, but I felt awe. She had been with Suzuki Roshi. I had read his book. It was so clear. I loved it and I hardly understood a word of it, but I felt peaceful when I read it and I felt his presence. He was dead. I'd never get to meet him, but here was Maggie Kress, who had known him. Whether we know it or not, we transmit the presence of everyone we have ever known, as though by being in each other's presence we exchange our cells, pass on some of our life force, and then we go on carrying that other person in our body, not unlike springtime when certain plants in fields we walk through attach their seeds in the form of small burrs to our socks, our pants, our caps, as if to say, "Go on, take us with you, carry us to root in another place." This is how we survive long after we are dead. This is why it is important who we become, because we pass it on.

I asked Maggie about Suzuki. She didn't say much. I realized then that when I'd asked anyone who'd known Suzuki about him, they hadn't said much. They smiled; they seemed to dream themselves to a place I couldn't see. What I had deciphered so far: He spoke English well, "for a Japanese person"; he liked to build rock gardens; he was funny.

I told her I sat meditation. She was generous. She offered me her guest cottage to do an all-day sit. Sassafras joined me on a Sunday. We made up a schedule of sitting and walking meditation, pledged to stay with it all day, and began. There were only the two of us the first time. That alone taught me a lot: You don't wait for a crowd to join you. You just do it and you feel thankful for the one person who does join you. The two of you together can turn the world around.

I don't know if I can tell what it is like to sit still all day— or even for one minute, for that matter—to have it broken only by the same tedious stillness of very slow walking meditation, and then back to sitting. Time goes so slowly that finally you surrender. You can't push the hours. Your mind creates ten thousand scenarios: wars with your mother, the bank, your best friend. Then love affairs with a chair, Hawaii, someone you met last week. And then for moments all that mental drama falls away and you're just sitting there, which is the scariest of all. There's just you and the person opposite you and your knees, your aching shoulders, the occasional eye blink and the breath that suddenly seems like a current of air rushing through you, filling your lungs like great sails. For one moment, my mind stopped. I was just present and a shuddering gratitude ran through me. Then Sassafras rang the bell—the bell! waves of sound—and there was a break for lunch. We sliced white cheese and spread mayonnaise and mustard on whole-wheat bread, sliced tomatoes, and ate these sandwiches, leaning back on cushions against the wall, our legs straight out in front of us.

We had made the rule that we were allowed to talk during lunch. Sass and I chatted. I noticed an old Xerox of a newspaper article on a shelf nearby. It was an interview with Allen Ginsberg. The title of the interview was "Polishing the Mind." I reached for it and began to read. Ginsberg talked about writing and the mind. It was the first time I'd heard someone talk about meditation and writing together. I decided right then to check out the possibility of studying with him. When I lived up at Lama, I'd heard he taught at Naropa Institute at the Jack Kerouac School of Disembodied Poetics. I loved that name for a school and repeated it often in my mind. The name sounded so ridiculous, like nothing I'd ever heard a school called before. It made me happy.

And then I did an extraordinary thing: I stole the article. There is no other way I can say it. I took it, put it in my purse, and knew I would keep it forever, that I would never give it back, that it was mine, it belonged to me. This is a terrible confession. Here was Maggie, who was a friend, who lent us her house to meditate in, and here I was stealing right in the middle of a meditation break. I could easily have asked her for it; I felt intuitively that she didn't care about it: It was old and in a pile of papers. I could have borrowed it, photocopied it and given it back to her. I could have done any number of appropriate things and I wish I had, but at the time the feeling of possession was so immediate, I never questioned its ethics. I didn't even think of it as stealing, there wasn't a moment of guilt. I feel awe as I write this, at how strong my direction and overwhelming my feeling was: I wanted to know, to have something I had just gotten a glimpse of. Under my sweet facade, I was ruthless.

I now realize, too, that when I left Lama in the fall I stole the first zafu (meditation pillow) I ever sat on. I instinctively felt it was mine. I just took it. Immediate, direct: I didn't do it sneakily. Meditation was mine. I took it joyfully, openly. I still own it.

One night a group of women gathered at Rosemary Ryan's house on Morada Lane to create a women's group. What form would it take? I stepped forward and said, "I'll teach a women's writing group and it'll be sixteen dollars for a round of eight weeks." I had no plan to propose that until I stepped forward, and I did it with such confidence that the women eagerly agreed. Before this group the only teaching of writing I had done was at the local hippie grade school. Most of the women traded with me for the class rather than paying me. I received fresh-baked bread, a hand-sewn pillow, even ten dollars worth of food stamps. I didn't really care, but somehow an exchange seemed important.

My experience in women's groups prior to this writing group was one of a profound resistance to leadership. Anything that smacked of hierarchy was tainted by the male system. But because I bloomed into this position as the teacher—it was natural, spontaneous—and because I suggested something everyone latently had a wish for, writing, there was no need for a struggle over authority, and everyone seemed happy to have a direction and the structured activity for the group that I provided. We all wanted to *do* something.

Teaching that group became a deep focus for my life. By the time I came to the meeting each week, I was brimming with ideas for writing topics. "Give me this moment," I would call out, and we would all dive into our notebooks wildly surprised and delighted at what came out. "Okay, now ten minutes on your grandmother's teeth." The pens would fly. I thought of writing as egalitarian, anyone could do it: If we spoke the language, if we learned to read and write in public school, if we had an arm to hold a pen, why just, "Go! for ten minutes." We would read our writing aloud immediately afterward. No chance for the editor to butt in. We were all eager to read aloud. There was so much support; no one felt ashamed or embarrassed of her own mind. I think I must have been electrical in those days. I believed in writing so much that everyone else believed in it, too. Though I was the only self-declared writer, everyone was happy to share writing with me. It gave my own work a focus and a direction.

The group took writing out of the realm of the lone individual aloft a mountaintop, pecking out granules of terse truth on a typewriter. We made writing communal, about relationship. We learned about each other. The aim was to glow, not to publish. And we discovered we glowed if we stayed connected to first thoughts, the first way our mind flashed on something. That was where the vital energy was and we learned together how to express it through original detail—the real details of our lives. And that's some of what Ginsberg talked about in his interview. Together we explored our dreams, first sexual experiences, obsessions, our mothers, our fears—nothing was off limits, because writing included everything.

Hari Dass, the Hindu guru I met at Lama, had a saying: "Teach in order to learn." In the writing group, we had all stepped outside the usual structure, so no one thought to ask on what authority I taught. Taos was like that then. It was okay to try something new and not be fabulous at it immediately. It was very tolerant of failure, which fostered beginners who would most likely fail a lot. You could learn to play a guitar one week, pluck out a few good songs, and the next week be on stage. It made for tremendous fresh energy.

At that same time, my friend Michael Reynolds began his experiments with solar homes made out of beer cans and old tires. He was sitting in a pyramid he had built out in a nearby town—not on any drugs—and five wizards appeared to him and dictated information that he wrote down in a notebook. It took him many years to digest and understand what they said about time and space and energy. These understandings went into his buildings. He was an architect with a degree from the University of Cincinnati. His architectural training did not include advice from wizards, but having moved to Taos, his vision under that big sky expanded. He let himself receive information from ethereal sources and he created sound homes with that information, homes built of recycled materials, that use no source of energy but the sun for heat and electricity. Now, seventeen years later, his buildings are called Earthships.

The breakdown of traditional ways of perception that was alive in the hippie generation and in the life of Taos allowed people to experiment with the seemingly ridiculous—building houses out of beer cans or having a writing group where everyone wrote together right there and then read their work aloud. There was even a sound therapy group I attended for a while. We called ourselves "The Screamers." I honor Taos for giving me and others that space.

When I returned to Taos years later, after *Writing Down the Bones* was published, I learned another thing about the place. Though it could accept failure, success was strange to it. Right after I signed a contract for my second book, I spoke with someone who had stayed in Taos for eighteen years. I was excited and blurted out, "I'm ready to go as far as I can, to go all the way. To get as good as I can be."

She paused. She was honest. She said, "I don't think I've ever heard anyone say anything like that before."

But Taos, those roots of freshness, is what we must come back to over and over again, no matter how successful we get.

Once the other women surprised me and borrowed a cabin from a friend in the ski valley. They blindfolded me and brought me up there for the weekend. We wrote all the time—on rocks by a stream, among wild strawberry patches, just ripened, on the wood deck of the house, leaning against aspens—and because it was summer, we enjoyed the freedom of sun on our bodies and no one else around. At night they made me a huge steak dinner, ordered the meat special from the market in El Prado.

Odd, now, to think of that steak—all of us were quite health-conscious—but I think it was symbolic, bacchanal, wild, not our usual way. We wrote and wrote.

"Throw out a topic," I'd say.

Jean said, "Kissing." We bent our heads over our notebooks and wrote madly for ten minutes.

"Another topic," I'd say.

"Green tea," Cecile yelled out. No discussion, we just jumped in and wrote again.

Then we read aloud, no editing, and we listened to each other, with no praise or blame.

Here is something I wrote during that weekend fourteen years ago that has survived:

> Listen!
> let's just decide to stay
> no one'll notice—
> really!
>
> the air's good
> your butts need exercise
> there's berries to be picked
> our backs bent over
> like stones in sun
>
> We make good meals
> Not a lot of flies
> We'll write books together
> great philosophy
> poetry
>
> I'll buy a green convertible
> we'll go tooling in the country

I don't like building
someone else will do it
I don't like working
someone else will earn the money

MONEY!
We!
We don't need money!

We have beautiful breasts
and souls
good sneakers
Roz has a fine hat
and socks we've got

We have everything!

("Eight Nude Women on Sunday in the Mountains," in
Chicken and In Love, Holy Cow! Press, Minneapolis: 1980)

That women's group did not end after eight weeks. It went
on for several years. Some people left; others joined us. No
matter who came and went, I was always there. Sometimes only
three people showed up for a certain evening. That was fine! I
taught anyway. For me there was no such thing as failure. I
loved it so much that if no one had showed up, I would have
talked to the chairs, the windows, the mountains, the trees
about writing practice. I was completely committed. This group
writing woke up something dynamic in me. I was unbeatable,
never discouraged. I set up a second women's writing group to
meet in the afternoons in my living room. We sat in a circle

on the floor with notebooks on our laps. Then I set up a third
one. I invited people over on a Saturday night—men, too—
and Neil, my boyfriend, and I would lead them in word jams.
One night we took off on the old jazz line, "Same old used to
be," and we went round and round, each person doing oral riffs
on that phrase. "Same old same old used to be the same, now
it's different but used to used to used to be old and then the
same . . ." All of us clapping and banging pots.

I did go to Naropa to study with Ginsberg. The summer after
I read that article I signed up for six weeks of classes, a poetics
course with Allen and a Buddhist lecture course taught two
evenings a week by Chögyam Trungpa Rinpoche, a Tibetan
meditation master. Rinpoche had escaped Tibet after the Chinese
invasion when he was twenty years old, leading hundreds of
people across the Himalayas to India. They boiled the leather
on their backpacks and ate it when the escape extended over
one mountain range after another and they ran out of food.
This impressed me.

Ginsberg's class was wonderful. He told us stories about
Jack Kerouac and what it was like to be a poet in the fifties.
He wanted us to understand the depth of the Beat generation
and how its poetry was serious, even scholarly, that it had a
link to all great poetry. What he said about writing he knew
from experience. He was a working writer. He knew rhyme
schemes and poetic rhythms that I had never heard of. He
always sat behind his desk in a nappy suit he told us, holding
up the lapel, he bought at the Salvation Army. We read Hart
Crane aloud, wrote ballads. I wrote a bawdy one and was
delighted by it. I'd never written a ballad before. I sang it to

myself as I rode a friend's bike around the tree-lined streets of Boulder.

Ginsberg had tremendous humanity. I remember being at the bar of the Boulderado Hotel, the Naropa hangout, when Ginsberg walked in. Someone half-drunk whom Allen had never met grabbed at his sleeve and said something surly about Ginsberg's fame. Instead of being annoyed, angry, or abrupt, Ginsberg turned to him and gently replied, "Yes, I am a poet. What would you like?"

Allen often had a lot of people over in his apartment for a meal. I remember I was there once, there were eight or ten of us at the table and he was encouraging us to eat—his lover of that time had made a big pot of soup—when there was a knock at the door. It was a Jehovah's Witness. Allen invited him in. "Eat, eat," he said and found him a chair and brought it over to the table. The evangelist was so stunned he did as he was told and spooned soup into his mouth. After a while, Ginsberg turned to him. "Now, what is it you came to tell me?"

Ginsberg was a deeply practicing Buddhist and his openness astounded me. Again, I was learning from the whole person, not from a lecture in front of a class.

I didn't stay in the Naropa dorms, which consisted of an apartment complex. I stayed at a college friend's brother's commune. As a matter of fact, he was the brother of Carol, my friend from Mr. Crane's classes, the woman with the crooked front tooth who ate caramel turtles. There was an extra room in the house and it was cheap.

By the end of the six weeks, I could pedal up the steep hill on Ninth Street every day without having to walk the bike. I spent a lot of time alone, sitting in a graveyard, leaning against a stone marker, writing. There was a "scene" at Naropa, would-

be writers hanging out around the stars, the published writers.
I didn't like most of the writing that was being done there. In
truth, I didn't understand it. I suspected that other people didn't
understand it either, but there was some wonderful encouragement—anything went; people could write what they wanted.
We were free, antiestablishment. This was in the third year of
Naropa's existence. It was a young place then and it generated
a lot of generosity. For hours one afternoon, Ginsberg wrote
spontaneous poems for a dollar apiece for a fund-raiser for the
school. We all stood in long lines to receive a poem.

Naropa was organic, alive. There was always the threat
that it could fold financially. This was good. Only something
alive can die. The public schools go on year after year. They
don't die because they are not alive. I remember a reading at
Naropa in a gymnasium with six hundred people cheering six
poets. In the United States, where poetry is not valued, this
was a marvelous experience.

I was quiet in Boulder and just watched everything closely.
I was on my way to trusting the texture of my own mind. Plus
I had the land of New Mexico, Taos Mountain, the Rio Grande
to rely on. These grounded me, kept me honest, were always
at my back, a standard for what was real.

Being in Boulder made me realize how I had fallen in love
with New Mexico. I had found a place that was mine. I realized
no day went by there that I didn't stop, take a breath and look
around. I'd never seen sky so big, so deeply blue. I'd watch the
big white cumulus clouds sail over Taos Mountain and then
wispy ones trail behind. I felt immense, limitless as the sky and
in the same moment felt unimportant, little—and that smallness
felt good, placed me properly in the dimension of life: I became
humble. This was my home, the beginning roots of my spiritual
life. I loved the modulated, often crumbling, soft adobe houses

the same color as the land, and the tall, pink hollyhocks against the brown walls. I noticed everything more in New Mexico— old rotted wood, the way mud dried, doors, gates, long dusty dirt roads, the mystical quality of Taos Mountain lost in a snowstorm, the hailstorms in late afternoon in August, the distant crack you saw in the land that you knew was the Rio Grande. I had a land I identified with and was connected to. This was important. I wasn't so easily tossed away.

Having a sense of place is a very affirming and steadying influence on a writer. If you learn to love one place, you are more aware of other places, can imbue your writing with that recognition of the importance of place. I heard someone say that place is the third character in a novel—that's how much power it has. Faulkner and Tennessee Williams cannot be separated from the South; Steinbeck belongs forever to California; Willa Cather eats Nebraska and the states below it; Carl Sandburg lives in Chicago; Edith Wharton has New York.

Recently in a writing workshop, I asked my students to write about their angels. My angels were places I not only loved but felt deeply about. Something had passed through me in those places: Norfolk, Nebraska, the large backyard vegetable gardens, the black turned earth, no fences from yard to yard, my friend's white house on the corner of Thirteenth Street, that street that stretches all the way from Canada to New Orleans, and the twenty-one-year-old man I fell in love with in Norfolk after I was divorced at thirty-four, how we ate popcorn in the movie theater on Sunday afternoon, only two other people in the whole place. A Midwest rain splashed the streets when we walked out. I had finally become an American.

Another angel of a place for me was New Albin, Iowa, one mile from the land the Minnesota Zen Center owned. I'd walk there early afternoons along the winding dirt road past

wild tiger lilies and red barns and go to the High Chaparral,
where Ellie Mae made the best fried chicken and peach pies,
and Herb, her husband, served drinks. I'd sit at a booth and
watch the local farmers bring in dead rattlers they killed after
finding them sunning themselves on flat white rocks high on the
bluffs along the nearby Mississippi. Each day Herb would ask
me, "So how's it going up at Boodie land?" and I'd sip a sweaty
Coke from the bottle with a straw and say, "Fine," and smile.
The train would go through the town and I'd hear its low sound.

Boulder, Colorado, was never one of my angels, though
my time there was rich. The land itself, the mountains that
surrounded the town were too dark, rough, rigid with narrow
canyons. In order to make a place my angel I had to feel I could
dream there, find a part of myself there and then carry that
place in me from then on. Not Boulder; too many malls, too
antiseptic, but because it was nothing, the land stepped back
and Rinpoche could step forward, bigger than Boulder, separate
from it.

Rinpoche traditionally came one or two hours late for his lectures. All three or four hundred of us waited, sitting on zafus,
in the big lecture hall. We surmised his lateness was a secret
teaching. We were naive then and thought everything a foreign
spiritual teacher did had a meaning. We never thought he came
late because he might be arrogant, rude, or drunk. All of the
above might have been true. We know now that Rinpoche was
alcoholic; he died about ten years later of complications probably
related to cirrhosis of the liver. But he was also a holder of the
crazy wisdom lineage of Tibet, the eleventh tulku of that line,
meaning the recognized reincarnation of the tenth, and he knew
something I could learn from. I accepted all the pomp and

circumstance around him and tried to understand what he was talking about. Mostly I didn't understand—either it was over my head or he wasn't clear in his communication, but teaching in the Eastern sense is different from the Western way. In the West, a teacher imparts knowledge to a student. In the East, a teacher transmits nothing more or less than his or her being. That is why we thought Rinpoche's coming late to class was part of a teaching. Even though I never got much out of what he said, there was something big in his presence that didn't have to do with words. So I let his words go over me the way one listens to the wind. I don't think, what is the wind saying?, I just let it blow over me and I hear its howl. I was hearing Rinpoche's presence. With Hari Dass, the guru I met the first week at Lama who hadn't spoken in twenty years, his presence was so extraordinary that I simply accepted him as out of this Western world. But here was Rinpoche, speaking English with an English accent—he was educated at Oxford—wearing a navy blue suit, a tie, and a white shirt, making fun of our promptness, holding a scotch in his hand. There still was some presence beyond his words that I felt I couldn't shake off.

At the end of my second week in Boulder, I stood and watched as people lined up after lecture to say a few individual words to Rinpoche and to be blessed by him. Suddenly I saw that he didn't really exist; he was fluid energy in the form of a man; there was nothing solid about him. I felt I could put my hand through him, as you can through sunlight coming in the window. I looked around. No one else seemed to see anything unusual. I looked back at him and I still saw him that way. It wasn't a moment's flash or illusion. I stood there for twenty minutes while he greeted everyone in line, and I watched the energy flow through him the whole time. Understand, I was not given to hallucination. Other than my heart opening in front of that sixth-grade class, nothing out of the ordinary had happened to me. Even my dreams were ordinary. My friends told me fantastical dreams about their bodies dissolving into the body of a blue heron. My dreams were on the order of: I go into a grocery store to buy a hot dog and a chocolate bar and I come out eating precisely those two things. And here I was viewing Rinpoche as ephemeral and I was certain it was true. I was standing with my two feet on the gymnasium floor. I wasn't drunk or high. I never said anything to anyone. It felt private, real, and it impressed upon me something beyond what we think human beings to be. I left the building, got on my bike, and pedaled home under the ten thousand stars.

Sassafras, my friend from Taos, who three months earlier had moved to Boulder and changed his name back to Richard Peisinger, saw me after the lecture, and then showed up at my house that evening. "What went on with you? It seemed like something was happening to you after lecture."

"Oh, nothing," I said. I wasn't lying. I didn't know what to say.

A few weeks later Rinpoche lectured on the three marks of existence: suffering, impermanence, and egolessness. Egolessness! Everyone is full of ego, I thought. I remember he laughed and said, "You don't understand it, but it is true. One mark of existence is the egolessness of existence." The rest of the lecture was terribly boring and long and I had trouble sitting still, but when it was over, I burst out crying, as though I had just heard an amazing thing that I knew was true and did not understand.

Then I left Boulder and returned to Taos. Our vegetable garden had grown in the six weeks I was gone. The basil leaves glinted in the sun, the buttercrunch lettuce were full heads now, and some of the radishes had already gone to seed. I loved Taos more than ever and knew that someday I would inevitably have to leave. Something was beginning to compel me. I was too young to be one of the best poets in Taos and I knew I needed a meditation teacher. I was afraid my ego would eat up all the sitting I did: I would toot my horn and think I was great or ignorant or use meditation as a measure of my value and take sitting away from just sitting. I was beginning to understand these things better. I sat my first ten-day meditation retreat in August, up at the Lama Foundation, with Jack Kornfield and Joseph Goldstein. This was 1976. I was twenty-eight years old.

In fall, the apricots fell ripe from the trees and we made pies and jams. The following summer I tore myself away from Taos and Neil and moved to Boulder. I became a student of Chögyam Trungpa Rinpoche.

All this while I continued to write. I tried hard to write with no aim, just to fill notebooks and to see what my mind turned up by itself without my trying to control it. This was very open space. It was the pathless path. I tried to stay directionless. Who was I really if I left my mind to its own devices? No poem, no novel, no essay; no trying to be deep or not deep, funny or not funny—or smart, intelligent, agile, beautiful, adept. Just write.

"I want to learn to do nothing," I repeated often in those years. What did I mean by that? After all, I was writing; I was meditating. I *was* doing something. I couldn't articulate it then, but I wanted to be empty of my attachment to things. I wanted to allow things simply to be, without my needs and projections. I noticed that the hippies were not only poor, nonmaterialistic; it was also their creed. They made poverty a virtue and became judgmental, critical of anything not like them. The Hispanics in the neighborhood, on the other hand, had always been poor.

They wanted to get out of their poverty. It was one of the things—that attachment to poverty—that caused conflict be-tween the two cultures.

Duality: it was a word I'd heard a lot in Buddhism. I saw it in myself: I'm a beginning writer and I want to become great; I'm over here and I want to go over there. Now I wanted to stop that. I wanted just to let writing unfold, no aim, no goal. I wanted to trust the natural goodness of my mind and life, that if I stopped worrying, manipulating, it would take me where I needed to go.

The end of duality does not mean we never do anything. It means we are empty of a need for result. So you raise a child to raise a child, not for your own needs and self-aggrandizement, not for power or desire, but just for the life of the child. You eat a meal for the goodness of being alive and needing nour-ishment and you feel the bite into that apple, that bread, that strawberry, and you let yourself feel all the effort and work of many beings to bring that food to this moment: the farmers, the sunlight, earth, water, truck, grocer. When we sink into the moment of just being, we lose our illusion of separateness, our ego. I think this is what Rinpoche meant by egolessness being a mark of existence. When I wrote and got out of the way, writing did writing. There was no me; just language and thoughts unfolding, and this did not feel good or bad; there was no me experiencing it one way or another.

In order to discover this I had to slow down tremendously. I had to be chewing the strawberry when I chewed the straw-berry, instead of chewing the strawberry and not being there, because I had my mind on my math exam or the comment my friend had made at lunch or worrying about how I could buy that silk blouse and also pay my water bill. I had to pay attention to the way the taste popped on my tongue, the way my jaw moved, my urge to swallow, my swallowing, my urge for another bite. And if I sank deeply into that attention I felt simultaneously the myriad beings and life run through me. And just as I chewed the strawberry when I chewed the strawberry, I wanted to write just to write, to be there.

I was outside American culture. I had stepped into Eastern mind. After all my years of Western education, I wanted to learn how not to think. The funny thing is you don't *learn* how not to think, you slow down and let thinking be thinking, walking be walking, crying be crying, dying be dying, and writing be writing. You are present where you are. I wanted to write out of another place than A leads to B and B to C. That logic was what I was taught in school, and I knew it was rare that anyone learned how to write in school.

When I ate that strawberry, I became one with it. Even if my attention only lasted for moments, that dissolution of myself, of my ego boundaries, felt truer than anything else I had experienced before. That same experience when I wrote, that dissolution of my ego boundaries, allowed me to join the lineage of writers. We were not separate. The simple act of moving my pen across the page linked me to all people past, present, and future who moved their pen across the page. The act of doing it connected me to a literary stream. It didn't matter what I wrote; all writers struggled with their minds and fears and blocks. I was one of them, just as I became a Buddha with all Buddhas who sat the moment I sat, crossed my legs, connected with my breath. There was no evaluation; good Buddha, bad Buddha. There was just Buddha, an awake being, someone who was present even if just for a moment.

When they're writing well, writers know all these things, or experience this nondualistic awake state, but no one has been able to articulate the writing path, so it does not get passed on and each writer individually has to luck out and bump into it. But even so, each of us must make that human effort, experience the writing path ourselves and so keep it alive. Jim White, my dear poet friend, said, "Poetry will never betray or abandon you, but you may abandon it." Poetry is always there, waiting for you to dip into it, just as the breath is always there (until it's not there and we're dead) waiting for us to notice it. No, not even waiting. Just there. We happen to notice it or not. We happen to connect with our own nature or not. I happened to discover writing from a whole new angle, from a fascination with the mind.

I wanted to learn to let go of thoughts and at the same time be mindful, full of mind, not mindless. Thoughts are like water bugs darting along the surface of the water, mostly unrooted, precarious. Usually we use thoughts to try to get control of a situation, even the situation of our own mind. These are called second and third thoughts, thoughts on thoughts. We have a raw, real root thought from the bottom of our mind—"I am going to die someday"—and instead of staying with that and feeling our fear or curiosity or whatever arises naturally, we grab that thought and try to choke it. "No, not me. No, I'm not. Let's not think about that. I'd like to buy a red car instead of a blue car." These are second and third thoughts. In writing we want to stay with first thoughts, that raw energy that comes from the bottom of the mind. In order to do that, we must embrace the whole mind, be mind-full.

What is mind, anyway? I think it's hard to define because from my experience it is everything. It is open space, no boundaries, no beginning or end, no past or future. It is our chance at eternity and infinity, but it means letting go of our small selves, the self that says, "Not me, I'm not gonna die." When we open to big mind, what I've called wild mind, we have to die to small mind. So, in a sense, each time we sit down to write we have to be willing to die, to let go and enter something bigger than ourselves. Wild mind includes writing with our whole body, our arms, heart, legs, shoulders, and belly. This kind of writing is athletic and alive. We must get out there in the playing fields of our notebook.

How do you enter wild mind? I don't think it's our job to worry about that or even to make that distinction. If we want to write, our job is to write, to surrender to our first thoughts, to write from our whole lives and to keep that hand moving, so that the whole lineage of writers rushes through us, like some great American river. Then let it be a great world river, too.

Recently I was in Lexington, Kentucky, for a women writers' conference. Lexington is in the heart of bluegrass country. Supposedly, it is the best place, besides Ireland, to raise thoroughbreds. In both places there are underground limestone caves that enrich the water with calcium, and that makes the horses' bones strong. I knew nothing about thoroughbreds before I went. While I was there I heard about Secretariat, Ruffian, brood mares, studs, the Triple Crown, and the Kentucky Derby. A former student drove me out to Keenland racetrack early one morning. That's when the horses work out, when the mist rises from that deep green grass. We drove through narrow country roads, past miles of long, white wood fences. We saw mares with their foals. I noticed how alive these animals were. Attuned to a simple movement, a car, a bird, a person, they pranced, darted across a field.

These thoroughbreds were bred for speed and all of them went back to three original horses in seventeenth-century England. They were the most beautiful animals I had ever seen. Their whole lives they were watched, trained, regulated to make the most of the power of their lineage. Under the skilled direction of a trainer, the thoroughbreds were able to become their full potential, what they were born for: to race. I stood in the bleachers, holding a steaming cup of hot chocolate, and watched, open-mouthed. Just then a trainer let out her horse at full speed. I couldn't believe its force, its immense moving muscular structure.

It was April, but unusually cold. My student's daughter was a trainer. She was twenty-nine years old. She'd fallen the year before. She was hurt badly, recovered, and was back on the horses.

"Do you worry about her?" I asked, taking a sip from my cup.

"There's nothing I can do. Once you're in this life, it's the only life. She just lives horses," my student told me and shrugged.

"Does she go out, have relationships?" I asked. I was trying to understand this life.

She smiled. "Nope. She doesn't have time, doesn't care. This is her life."

We had to leave Keenland to get back to my workshop on time. There were about eighty people in the class, most of them from the area. A lot of them didn't care about horses, but one person told me about a man who had requested that his ashes be scattered on Ruffian's grave. "She was an incredibly fast filly, broke her leg racing at Belmont, and had to be put away."

"Belmont?" I said. "In New York?" My father went to Belmont, I thought to myself. You mean these gorgeous animals were connected with betting and bookies, were connected with my childhood?

After the workshop, another student took us out to Claibourne, the thoroughbred farm where Secretariat was buried. He was one of the great racehorses of all time. We went to his grave. He was buried in an eight-foot mahogany coffin with a gold satin lining.

My student told me, "They don't usually bury the whole horse, but he was special. Hundreds of people came to his funeral."

"Well, what do they bury if they don't bury the whole horse?" I asked.

"Most horses they don't bury at all. With the real winners, they bury the head, the hooves, and the heart," she told me nodding.

"The heart?" I asked, astonished.

"Yes, that's what a horse runs with: his heart. That's what they say, that horse has heart. If they've got heart, it makes up for other things, they can still win," she explained.

Why was I so fascinated? As I left Lexington, I came out of my thoroughbred trance. I thought to myself, my god, this is terrible. There are people starving all over the world and some of these horses auction for a million dollars. But what caught me, I think—what was at the center of this thoroughbred industry, beyond the buying and selling—was big mind, the tremendous power and radiance of these animals, their concentration and oneness when they race, and the dedication of the people close to them. I thought to myself, this is how we have to write, with that kind of heart, with that dream of racing, of using our whole body, with the depth of those green fields, with that singlemindedness, that fullness of the whole mind, the whole being.

When I moved to Boulder I took refuge in the triple treasure: the Buddha, the dharma, and the sangha. I took refuge in the belief that Buddha was a human being and that we are all capable of being in that awake state. I took refuge in the dharma, the teachings of the Buddha, and in the sangha, the spiritual community of other people on the path. And what does it mean to "take refuge"? It means we can't do it alone, we need a shelter. It does not mean we diminish ourselves— "I'm helpless." Rather, we are connecting, coming out of isolation. We are connecting with real support, not with a career or with our boyfriend or girlfriend, but with the real support of wisdom. By committing ourselves to the teachings, we are committing ourselves to ourselves, because the practice brings out our true self.

Rinpoche made sure to tell us that after the refuge ceremony every cell in our bodies would become Buddhist and that from then on we would be refugees, which meant there was no final home, no place we could rest; life, after all, was impermanent.

For me, a Jew, it felt true. My people were always refugees. And as an American, too, it felt true. We were a restless lot.

The people who had signed up to take refuge stood in line at twilight outside Rinpoche's office. We went in singly, stood in front of his desk, told him our name, and he bent over a white piece of paper and wrote our dharma name in Tibetan calligraphy. This was our new name signifying our entrance into

Buddhism. Our dharma name was supposed to be our basic energy. I guess he intuited it as we stood in front of him. I didn't know much about this stuff. He started writing as soon as I walked in. There was a wild painting of a dragon hanging on the wall behind him. Two men in gray suits stood at attention on either side of the painting as if to guard Rinpoche. I recognized both of them as his senior students. He was wearing a navy blue suit again, and his dark Tibetan skin also looked navy blue; again I saw him as ephemeral, just for a moment. There was so much warmth emanating from him, I wanted to linger forever by his side.

The next week was the ceremony. I bought a new dress, blue with splashes of pink flowers. We sat on zafus. There were twenty of us. Rinpoche sang a Tibetan song and threw white rice, which hit the highly waxed wooden floor and then bounced before it settled—just like rain on a sidewalk. I was married now to Buddhism and I knew I was also a Jew—I couldn't wash that skin away—and I was also an American, a feminist, a writer. I felt no contradictions. Buddhism never asked me to deny anything I was. I knew I would always live at the edge of many worlds. I felt large enough in that moment to encompass them all. I received the refuge name "Wind Lake of Enlightenment." It was a beautiful name. I liked it and didn't know what it meant.

Buddha became awakened sitting under the bodhi tree, when he glanced up and saw the first morning star in India, and twenty-five hundred years later in Boulder, Colorado, a whole bunch of us entered his path, but Buddha was Buddha. I had to make my own human effort to realize now what it meant to be a human being on earth; I had to come to my own clear vision. His existence told me it was possible. The dharma, the teachings, gave me some footholds, but now I was on my own with my own soupy, amorphous life that sometimes felt like I was engineering a bowl of Jell–O and trying to give it direction.

A man I knew, Joshua Zim, who earlier had lived at the Lama Foundation and then moved to Boulder to be with Trungpa, told me once that Trungpa had stood at the top of a murderous flight of stairs at 1111 Pearl Street and called down to Zim, "Are you ready?" and when Zim hesitated for an instant, Trungpa threw himself down the stairs. Zim leaped to catch him midway, at the landing, and tore his sportscoat on the banister. Zim said what Trungpa was asking was, was he ripe, ready to be awakened. To help him, to startle him out of his usual way, Trungpa was even willing to risk his own life. Zim felt totally bewildered and dejected and said that he hoped he would get another chance someday.

"Sure," Trungpa said, and plunged down the remaining steps, to Zim's complete surprise.

Refuge was as far as I went with Chögyam Trungpa Rinpoche—I never caught him flying down a flight of stairs. I wasn't very ripe, I knew that, more like the beginning bud of a peach blossom, which a long time later might become a peach, if a late spring frost or hailstorms didn't get me first.

Nine months after I moved to Boulder, I left for Minneapolis to get married. Neil, the man I had been with since Taos, wanted to move there. It was his hometown and he could work for his father. I was too much in love not to go with him. He went ahead and I followed a few months later. As I drove my car across Nebraska, I remembered what the palm reader outside of Albuquerque had said a long time before: "You're going to go some place you've never been before. Where you know no one. Into the deep north. You'll do this for the love of a man."

Minnesota was certainly as far north as I had ever been.

PART
THREE

I knew no one in Minneapolis when I moved there except Neil, the man I was going to marry. I was thirty years old. We had a small wedding in my father-in-law's backyard. The wedding cake was chocolate. I liked that. The trees were deep green—it was late spring—and the sky was gray. During our marriage ceremony, a vase of gladioli fell over. I wore a gardenia in my hair, and as the judge spoke our vows, I heard a semi rumbling in the distance.

That summer was humid, full of mosquitoes. We lived in the lower half of a house in the Cedar-Riverside area, an old hippie and radical student ghetto. A Mr. Steak sign blinked across the street next to a Mobil gas station where I went to purchase chewing gum. Down the block was a Pontillo's pizzeria.

I spent the first months in Minnesota in a daze, walking to the North Country food coop, down cement streets, past St. Mary's Hospital, Augsburg College, and brick and shingled duplexes. Electric pink petunias grew all over the place, and peonies, zinnias, columbines—I learned all their names. This was a civilized place, square lawns, gardens along house foundations, one-way street signs, posters for concerts and performances stapled to telephone poles. I could hear the hum of Interstate 94 nearby and a few blocks away was the Mississippi River. The Mississippi River! I thought. Home of America and Huck Finn. I walked there often, staring down at it, trying to make it more than a river, trying to give it the essence of why my grandfather packed up and left Russia for these United States.

Before I moved to Minnesota, I had heard that there was

a Zen center with a Zen teacher in the Twin Cities. People in Boulder told me the teacher's name was Katagiri Roshi. A few knew him, said he was strict—and good. I gulped. Zen? I had heard it was hard, austere, tough. The colors were black and white. Zen was Buddhism from Japan. The meditation room in Boulder had gold and orange and red. It reflected the Tibetan culture.

Eventually, for Buddhism to take root in the United States, it would have to become American Buddhism. That would evolve slowly. It would grow to include feminism, gay and lesbian culture, psychology, apple pie, African-American spirituals. It would be up to us to figure out what was essentially American, what was culture, and what was Buddhism, to taste its essence beyond Tibetan or Japanese culture, but first we had to sink into Buddhism in the culture it had lived in. Japanese and Tibetan cultures came with Buddhism to America; they were inseparable. You could not pull Tibet out of Chögyam Trungpa Rinpoche, yet he had adapted to America. He wore suits, spoke English, drove a car. In his very body, Tibetan Buddhism was moving slowly over into American Buddhism, because he had planted his body on American soil.

For me, Buddhism was Buddhism. I wasn't interested in the cultural part. I just wanted it; a light had been lit. I wanted to do formal sittings with other people. This determination was important when I moved to Minnesota. I didn't say to myself, "Well, I don't know. I like Thailand. I want to study Thailand's Buddhism," or, "Gee, I took refuge with Trungpa. I'll be with him forever, stay loyal even though he is a thousand miles away and I can't study directly with him," or, "I don't know. I'll see just how hard this Katagiri Roshi is. If it's too hard, I don't want to do it." I wasn't fussy about the form. I trusted in something essential about it.

I've watched meditation students come and go. They use anything as an excuse—"My knee hurt," "The teacher said *he* instead of *she*," "The schedule just wasn't good for me." There is no excuse: If you want it, go for it. Don't let anything toss you away. The other extreme is to accept blindly everything a teacher does: He's sleeping indiscriminately with the women in the community and you think, "Well, it's part of the teachings." It is best to stay alive, alert, trust yourself, but not give up, no matter what the situation. Get in there, stay in there, figure it out. If we want the teachings we have to let ourselves be hungry. If a green pepper is offered, eat it. If it's steak, devour it. If it's something indigestible—a turd, a cement block, a shoe—figure out what to do with it, but don't back away.

It is the same for writing. Some people write for fifteen years with no success and then decide to quit. Don't look for success and don't quit. If you want writing, write under all circumstances. Success will or will not come, in this lifetime or the next. Success is none of our business. It comes from outside. Our job is to write, to not look up from our notebook and wonder how much money Norman Mailer earns.

Just the fact that Katagiri was called "roshi," Zen master, meant that his authority had been bestowed upon him. This helped me to trust him as a teacher. He was connected to a lineage that reached all the way back to Shakyamuni Buddha. He didn't just wake up one morning and say, "Okay, now I'm a Zen master." He had training; he was on solid ground. His position was not based on his individual human ego.

There have been many self-declared gurus in America. On what basis do they anoint themselves? A momentary flash into the cosmos? It takes a lot of work and a foundation to maintain a deep insight in your daily life and then be able to transmit it to your students, but America is hungry and we often don't care about quality. We are quick to make someone a teacher. There are individuals with tremendous charisma, but unless they are rooted, grounded in a lineage, unless they are connected and answerable to other people, that energy can go amok. Hitler had charisma; so did Charles Manson. But it was unrooted and, therefore, dangerous. Rajneesh, who owned a hundred Rolls Royces and had a community in Antelope, Oregon, probably had a deep enlightenment experience, but he didn't back it with practice, a way to digest it in his daily life, a way to transmit it to all his cells moment by moment. It wasn't grounded.

I didn't know whether I'd like Katagiri—that didn't seem important to me, my individual likes and dislikes. I knew that he knew something, and that if I surrendered, didn't fight the form of the teaching, I could learn something. He was tough? I'd learn the tough form of Buddhism. Of course, I didn't understand all this that first day I encountered him, but just as with writing, I wanted something and wasn't sure of what it was I wanted. I just had energy, a direction, and determination.

On a Thursday morning three weeks after I moved to Minneapolis, I looked up the address of the Minnesota Zen Meditation Center in the telephone book: 3343 East Calhoun Parkway. I copied the address on a slip of paper and stuck it in my pocket. I was standing in our black-and-white linoleum kitchen. The kitchen cabinets were white, but held darker shadows. The sky was still gray outside. I learned that the Midwest had predominantly gray days. I walked to the corner bus stop at Twenty-fifth and Riverside, and when the bus pulled up, I told the driver, "I want to go to Zen Center."

"What?" he said. He had red hair, brown eyes, and was clean-shaven.

"Zen Center," I articulated. I naively thought everyone would know about it; after all, even people in Boulder knew about Katagiri.

He shook his head. "Never heard of it."

I pulled the address out of my pocket. "Here it is."

"Oh," and he explained the buses and transfers I had to take. It was on the other side of town, a long way away by bus.

I stepped down from the bus and walked home. This wasn't going to be a casual trip. I called Zen Center on the phone. They told me Roshi lectured on Wednesday evenings and Saturday mornings. I decided to drive over there on Saturday. I would go over the route with my husband. I was having a terrible time with the Twin Cities' freeways. The day before, I had been lost for an hour only ten minutes from our house. I was looking for the Minneapolis public schools' head office. I needed a job and was once again trying teaching. As I got in the car, I remembered my mother's constant encouragement for me to get a teaching certificate in college, because it was "a good job for a woman, something you could always fall back on." Here I was, suddenly doing what she had said.

Zen Center was an old house on Lake Calhoun. There was no sign outside, just a number. I went in through the back door, walked downstairs to the basement where you took off your shoes and hung up your coat, and then came upstairs to what used to be a big living room when it was a single family dwelling. Now it was a zendo, a formal place to do zazen, a form of sitting meditation where you let go of thinking and return to the present moment.

The walls were bright white, the floors bare wood with black cushions aligned in rows. I followed someone else who bowed, then entered the room. I bowed, then found a cushion to sit on. I looked around. There was a small wooden altar with a small statue of Buddha and two narrow glass vases of sweet peas with one purple columbine on either side of the statue.

The room was quiet. I heard footsteps on stairs, then Katagiri Roshi appeared at the entryway in black robes, bowed, and went to the altar. He lit incense, did three full prostrations on a brown zabuton, a soft mat, in front of the altar, and then sat down on a zafu. A bell was rung; we lifted white chant cards and chanted how wonderful and rare it was to hear the dharma, and that we should listen and remember it.

Then Katagiri began to speak. He was vibrant and seemed to be beaming, even though he wore a serious expression. I think even then, the first time, I noticed how beautiful his feet and hands were.

I listened hard to what he talked about; I didn't understand it, but it felt true. I remember I even asked a question at the end. He turned his head, smiled sweetly, answered it, and I still didn't understand anything. I left and felt like a motor in idle.

I went a few more times. I still only understood a few things Roshi said, and there was no one else to explain anything. I got the sense that you shut up, sat, bowed, drank tea, took off your shoes, chanted the Heart Sutra: No eyes, no ears, no nose, no tongue, no body, no mind; no color, no sound, no smell, no taste, no touch. I never heard the Heart Sutra before. It seemed odd. What the hell did it mean? I had a tongue and I had a body. Form is emptiness, emptiness itself is form. It seemed peculiar to me, but I found myself curious, intrigued. What's going on here?

In the second lecture I went to, Roshi kept repeating,

"Mountains are mountains. Mountains are not mountains. Mountains are mountains."

"What were they when they weren't mountains?" I asked. Everyone laughed. I was serious. I was trying to figure this out.

Roshi answered me, but I don't remember the reply. I don't remember it because I didn't understand it. I didn't understand anything: You could donate money for the lectures or not donate money. You could pay monthly dues or not pay monthly dues. You could come to Zen Center or not come. You could volunteer to help with a rummage sale or not volunteer, and everything was black and white, black and white. Even when Roshi lectured, everyone sat in zazen, their legs crossed, their hands linked together in their laps. They looked straight ahead, not at him, and even though sometimes he was hilariously funny—he'd talk about how to eat a pickle silently— no one laughed. A few smiled enigmatically.

I called Zen Center one day and asked for an appointment to see Roshi for an interview. Roshi answered the phone, said to come over that afternoon. I dressed up and drove there. Now I knew the route. Take 94 west to Hennepin, left on Hennepin to Thirty-fourth, down that to dead end, park, walk through alley to Zen Center, and enter through back door. Roshi came down the stairs for the interview wearing jeans and a green tee-shirt that said, "Marcy School is purr-fect." His younger son went there. I had nothing really to say to him. I think I was looking for a spark, some action, an entry in. I think even more I wanted some recognition. I wanted him to be interested in me. I wanted some attention.

This was the hardest part for me. You came and went at Zen Center and no one paid attention. No one asked me if I was going to return or told me they were delighted to see me. I was alone again; it was just like writing. There was no one over my shoulder cheering me on as I wrote. It all had to come from within.

"I wanted to know if you would be my teacher," I said to Roshi.

"Yes," he nodded.

That was it. That was too easy. No struggle. No demands. No fight. How could he say yes? He doesn't know me, I thought. How could I ask? I don't know him. I wasn't sincere about it. I didn't know what it meant to be sincere about it. I didn't know what it really meant to be a student or to have a teacher. Yet, often we are not connected with the depth of what we are doing or how sincere our hearts are. Something had bloomed in me in front of that sixth-grade class back in Albuquerque and it was continuing almost on its own.

We think we know what's going on, that we have control of our lives; we make plans, have date books and schedules, and then we turn around to see ourselves and realize our lives have their own composition, their own movement. Just recently I had this experience: I had planned for six months to go this December to India and as my brain made a budget and travel plans I noticed my body was moving toward being at Taos Pueblo for Christmas Eve. I even heard myself say to a friend in California, "Yes, I'll be here over the New Year," as though a part of my life moved in its own dream. I did consciously, finally, drop the idea of going to India in an instant one afternoon as I put a bag of groceries in the back seat of my car. Suddenly, it seemed obvious. I wasn't going. Nothing in me wanted to go this December except my head.

In the same way, I lived my life in Minneapolis consciously trying to adjust to the Midwest, to buying a kitchen table for our duplex, to a marriage that was no longer in the hippie world—suddenly this man I had slept with for years was my husband and he had a full-time job, he left every morning for work. And at the same time the dream of my life was moving like a huge ocean in unfathomable waves. I had just asked Katagiri Roshi to be my teacher; and though I wasn't aware of it, it was a deep request.

After a moment with nothing else to say to Roshi, I left and almost forgot about speaking with him, except for a thin strand of embarrassment, its color green, that I could glimpse out of the corner of my eye. I was embarrassed because somehow I knew I had been arrogant. I didn't know then how to meet Roshi eye to eye in an ordinary way. It was a big yes he responded with, though he did it quietly, quickly, directly. He was smart. He embraced all possibilities: that I might drop him the next day like a hot tomato or flower twenty years hence as a great Buddha. (He did actually tell me years later his response to that meeting: "I thought to myself, oh, she's a stubborn one.")

The next time I met with Roshi, I was going to interview him for the Zen Center newsletter. Nancy James, the editor, had called and asked me if I would do the interview. She thought it would be a chance for me to get to know him. I agreed to do it, but I wasn't very interested: Roshi had yet to captivate me. The morning of the interview, I woke up obsessed with what color material to get for curtains. After all, I had just gotten married and we were making a home for ourselves.

I drove to Zen Center to interview Roshi with that curtain obsession blazing in my mind. I planned to get the interview over with and then rush to the fabric store.

I parked in front of Zen Center and dashed out of the car. I was a few minutes late. I was halfway up the walk when I realized I'd left my notebook on the front seat. I dashed back to the car, grabbed the notebook, and ran to the back entrance of Zen Center. I flung open the door, spun around the corner, and came to a dead stop: Roshi was standing in the kitchen by the sink in his black robes, watering a pink orchid. That orchid had been given to him three weeks before. Someone had brought it from Hawaii for a Buddhist wedding I had attended. It was still fully alive.

"Roshi," I said in astonishment and pointed at the orchid.

"Yes." He turned and smiled. I felt the presence of every cell in his body. "When you take care of something, it lives a long time."

My mouth fell open. Suddenly, I didn't know anything, but for a moment I knew I didn't know anything, and that was a great opening. This human being before me was present. We could say, "Be here now," my generation, but I'd never encountered anyone before who was present, so I'd never had a real vision of what that meant. Roshi was just there, every cell of him. His foot wasn't back in his childhood, thinking about his grandfather's green Plymouth; his chin wasn't remembering how good that sugar cookie tasted a week ago. All of him was gathered in this moment and concentrated on the flower before him. That kind of presence was like a brick wall and I slammed against it, shattering all my disparate parts: the yellow curtains, my marriage, the Minneapolis expressway, my upbringing, my years of sitting in Taos, my notebooks and poetry; all went rolling on the floor.

We sat down at the kitchen table and I asked him the questions Nancy James had asked me to ask. He was funny. When he couldn't remember some information, he banged his head with his hand, as if to get that machine—his brain—working. I remember I paid a lot of attention to his arm. His arm seemed so vital, radiant. It was all there. I never thought of an arm as not being there before, but this arm had life in it.

Later a dancer at Zen Center told me that one evening she came to a lecture because a friend wanted to come. She said she didn't know what Roshi was talking about but that his presence was everything she tried to achieve as a dancer. She kept coming back and eventually became a Zen student.

That morning interview with Roshi was my true meeting with him. The gap closed between my conscious and unconscious mind. I saw who he was, a glimpse of him anyway; all of me saw it. Though even then I didn't know what it was, I knew it was good to be that startlingly present. And in seeing it, that possibility awoke in me. I had a vision of something whole.

In his list of essential rules for writers, Jack Kerouac wrote: "Be submissive to everything, open, listening." I could easily have missed who Katagiri was if I hadn't put myself in a position to go back over and over again. I understood that I was not "submissive to everything," and that I often missed something good because of my ignorance, so I would persist at something for a long while until I tasted it. It was hard for me to see something outside myself, but I had a glimpse of my basic ignorant sleepiness and if I sensed some essential rightness I would continue even though I didn't get it right away. I knew, like steel striking a flint over and over again, eventually something in me would be ignited, and I had a flash understanding of something real.

This was my attitude toward literature, too. If a play, poem, novel was centuries old, and I was bored reading it, I did not trust my boredom and think, this writing is no good.

I figured that if it had managed to last this long, it had something worth lasting. I'd wait until I either connected with it or a teacher helped shine some light on it. That's why a teacher is so important. A teacher can hold up a seeming piece of coal and point out the diamond.

There was a teacher, George Doskow, at St. John's Graduate Institute in Santa Fe, who opened Homer's *Iliad* for me one evening. I had been laboring alone to read it in my little cubicle of a dorm room. The verses bounced off my mind. I couldn't absorb them. Who cared about Achilles? He had nothing to do with me. I never fought a battle or knew a Trojan—who were they anyway? Then suddenly on a Wednesday night in a seminar class, with Doskow's help, I saw the wild heroism of Achilles at the moment just before he is about to go into battle. His best friend has just been killed by Hector, a Trojan, and Achilles breaks out of his frozen refusal to fight. In class I began to see the whole thing, the power and the pain, the huge sky behind him—he stands on a hill, I'm with him, I feel an ancient, wild glory as he turns from his stubborn feud with Agamemnon over the slave girl. That turning became forceful, exciting, because Doskow helped me to see it. The *Iliad*, that old book, became alive for me that night with real human emotion, with endurance and suffering. There was no distance anymore between me and the Greeks, that culture over there in Europe that touched the Mediterranean, a place I had never been, many centuries before I was alive on this earth. I remember that moment even now. Yes, I thought, yes. This story came thundering down to me through the ages. Now it was mine.

There at St. John's I began to trust my mind. We read only original texts in translation, no criticism or comments by scholars. We tried to meet directly the minds of those old writers who were the foundation of Western civilization. I had not yet begun to write; I had day-dreamed through college, and when I graduated, suddenly I woke up. I wanted to take an active part in my education, to learn something. During my four years as an undergraduate, I was still under the lethargic spell of my family. My father paid all the bills for me while I was in Washington; I paid my own way at St. John's.

Going to St. John's was also how I discovered New Mexico. When I first arrived in Albuquerque and looked out the airplane window, I saw those bald rugged Sandia Mountains casting a pink haze against that blue sky and I thought I had landed on another planet. I remember taking a shuttle to Santa Fe and being dropped off at the foot of Monte Sol. I was holding two suitcases, one in each hand, and a man in a green cap, his legs stretched out in front of him, was sitting on a bench.

"Is it always like this?" I asked him.

"Like what?" he said.

I turned all around, my mouth hanging open, and then I looked directly up overhead at a raven circling above me. "Is it always this clear, this big?"

"Oh, that," he said casually. "Yeah, I guess it is."

I put down my suitcases and stood there for a long time, looking, being quiet, digesting a whole new vision of earth and of the color blue for sky.

I connected with Socrates at St. John's, too. But this time it was without a teacher. I met him in my small dorm room one late night when I was reading *Phaedrus* over and over again. Finally, something from the dim and distant past penetrated me, and I felt Socrates enter my room. I felt his humanness, his wisdom. My heart was touched, almost as if a mist had wafted in from under my dorm room door, and I became saturated with light. I forgot all the discourses I didn't understand. I felt the soul of Socrates. That was all I needed. I accepted him into my life. He was no longer foreign, distant, classical. He was a real human being who had lived. There was no dichotomy, struggle, conflict between him and me anymore. After that I just received his work.

I also struggled with Immanuel Kant, *The Prolegomena to Any Future Metaphysics*—oh, was he difficult, just the title was enough to stump you. One day in class we realized his theory wasn't sound: It had a chink, a crack, it was more something he wished for humanity than a solid thought—and I laughed out loud, "My god! Manny, you're just a dreamer after all." My kind heart opened to him then. I don't think I ever read Kant again, but he and I had communicated for a moment.

Then one day a tutor (we called all the teachers "tutors," no one had a special rank) came late for evening class because, as he explained, "My wife is out of town, so I had to go out for dinner." Everything exploded for me with that statement. St. John's had taught me well the steps of logic—the year before I had put Darwin's theories into Euclidian theorems for my science thesis—and I leaped at the misplaced logic of my tutor's statement. "What did your wife's being out of town have to do with you filling your belly? Are you making the absolute statement that only your wife can cook? That is faulty reasoning. You, too, can cook!" Feminism burned in me from that moment on. Before that I'd read *Sexual Politics*, by Kate Millett, and *The Feminine Mystique*, by Betty Friedan, but now I felt sexism viscerally. In my class, a place where we supposedly examined propositions, this teacher (it was not Doskow) threw out a faulty one, "Only wives can cook," and I picked it up in my body and raged.

The rest of the semester I didn't care about the classics. I was busy listening for any false move one of the tutors might make: Calling humankind "mankind," and assuming that the word "*man*kind" included me, or saying "he" and forgetting "she." I knew I made the tutors nervous. Suddenly the attention had shifted from Aristotle to them, and I wanted to know where the women were in Western civilization. These male authors could no longer speak for me. Where were the women, and how come there were all male tutors? My friendships with Homer, Manny, and Socrates aside, I wanted to read women. Soon after I graduated with a master's degree, certifying my knowledge of "Western mind," I had that opening in front of that sixth-grade class. When I found meditation, the West took a landslide, fell off the earth for me. It was then that I realized they also forgot to mention Eastern culture at St. John's. Also African-American culture, Native American, Hispanic.

All my classics textbooks somehow ended up on my family's bookshelf in the TV room. My family mostly read newspapers, so it didn't matter what was on the bookshelf. When my parents retired to Florida, Descartes, Plato, Kant, Aristotle went with them and now sit unread below the ceiling fan, while the palm and hibiscus trees wave slowly outside the windows. My family probably has the finest collection of the classics in their entire condo complex.

Peter, a man I had met in Boulder before I moved to Minnesota, told me that in the late sixties he'd just gotten out of jail for being a heroin addict and was living in San Francisco on Page Street, just across from the San Francisco Zen Center. "One morning," he said, "I stepped out of my door and I saw Katagiri walking down the street. I didn't know his name then, but I knew he was from Zen Center; he was wearing those black robes. I just saw his back, then he turned the corner. I never saw a back that straight before. I watched it. I stood there a moment after I could no longer see it. Then I crossed the street, went in, and asked them to teach me how to sit. I've been doing it ever since. It was that back." And he shook his head.

Someone was teaching with his back? This was very different from St. John's. The presence of someone's back inspired someone else to become a meditation student? Yes. Zen is a body practice. It is taught through the body—you sit down in the zazen position and shut up—and your body is present whether your mind is or not. The teachings are transmitted through your body. Zen comes from Japanese culture. In Japan you don't ask questions: You learn by following an example, by imitating someone ahead of you. You keep quiet and pay attention and the learning penetrates your whole life, seeps into all your pores. Zen is not taught the way most of America's schools teach, from the neck up.

Here is something I like very much from the *Shobogenzo*, Dogen's lifework. Dogen is Japan's foremost religious thinker and philosopher.

MOUNTAINS AND WATERS SUTRA

There are mountains hidden in treasures. There are mountains hidden in swamps. There are mountains hidden in the sky. There are mountains hidden in mountains. There are mountains hidden in hiddenness. This is complete understanding.

An ancient buddha said, "Mountains are mountains, waters are waters." These words do not mean mountains are mountains; they mean mountains are mountains.

Therefore investigate mountains thoroughly.

When you investigate mountains thoroughly, this is
the work of the mountains.
Such mountains and waters of themselves become wise persons and sages.

(translated Arnold Kotler and Kazuaki Tanahashi,
in *Moon in a Dewdrop: Writings of Zen Master Dogen*,
North Point Press, 1985)

What? "These words do not mean mountains are mountains; they mean mountains are mountains." We aren't going
to understand this with our brains. The moment we hear it, we
think, yes, yes, I've got it, and then it fades. The only way to
understand it is with our whole body, to enter it, live it.

There are koans in Zen that are actually meant to trick
the mind, to crack it open, to break it from its habitual way of
understanding the world. We've all heard them: What is the
sound of one hand clapping? What is your original face before
you were born? a Zen master might ask you. These cannot be
answered in some usual way, because the question is not usual.
One person might answer, "A dog was my original face," and
have passed the koan, and another person might say, "A dog,"
and the roshi would tell him to go sit some more. One person
might pick up a stick and throw it into the air and pass the
same koan that another person who barks like a dog fails. But
this "passing" of a koan does not mean, "Great, I passed third
grade. I'm on to fourth." There's no getting ahead. To pass a
koan is to receive another koan, is to practice being in the
present moment, to settle into it, to deepen your experience of
here and now.

It is the presence of our minds when we answer the koan
that matters, and our minds are not just our brains trying to

figure out the right answer, our minds are all of us: our muscles, teeth, past, present, future, feet, stars, and earth. One with all of it. Then any way we respond is the answer. And answers and questions melt away. Dissolve. Just you. Here. And who are you? When we stop, really stop, who knows? I can tell you I'm Natalie. I can tell you all sorts of things about myself. That is not me, here, now. Me, here, now, I can't catch. Here, now, I'm nothing.

This Zen business from Japan is a very different way of being taught from the way Mr. Doskow, or even my beloved Mr. Clemente or Mr. Cates taught. My formal education in school and in society was to build me up, to teach me about culture, to give me a past, hopes for the future, to show me how to add ten and two dollars together to see if I have enough money to purchase a baseball bat. It was to give me identity, solidarity, meaning. Death, that obliteration we all must face, was never mentioned; sickness was not addressed.

Zen teaching tears our identity down, but it is not mean. It's tough. It asks us to slow down and examine who we are. Who is that "I" we walk around with, have developed, that has a body capable of contracting disease and is impermanent?

This, too, is helpful for writing. A writer needs to know death is at her back; otherwise, the writing becomes brittle, full of fear. Acceptance of death informs our writing with a much larger dimension. It becomes panoramic, encompassing everything. This does not mean we have to mention death by name all the time in our writing; we just have to know it exists in our bodies. Then that knowledge will naturally be transmitted in our work. It will make our work glow and be truly alive.

A friend who is a visual artist gave her aunt a drawing she did of columbines. Her aunt hung it in her bedroom, and during long hours of sickness—she was undergoing treatment for cancer—she would look at the pen and pencil drawing.

Susan, my friend, visited her a month later. Her aunt looked up from her bed. "You know, Susan, there's something wrong with those flowers. They're pretty, but they look like they're going to live forever. They're frozen. They're not real enough."

The columbines didn't have the knowledge of death, that fact of a flower's brief life that makes it all the more beautiful. I know Susan. She has trouble keeping still. She is a restless person. Being still in drawing, writing, or meditation is what allows our life to drop down to its bottom line—so we touch nothing, touch death as we draw, and our drawing can be filled with life.

Peter, the man who saw Roshi's back, also said to me, "I'd go study with Katagiri up in Minnesota, but I can't stand the cold."

The Minnesota cold. I moved to Minnesota in late spring and had a full humid green summer to enjoy. Everyone talked about the winter, but I couldn't believe it could be that bad. They must be exaggerating, I thought, but it got colder and colder until on December second it hit twenty below and continued that way. It rarely went above zero. Every snow that fell stayed and created another crusty layer not to melt until spring, and spring didn't come until late April. We had to plug our car in to keep the motor oil warm. There were mornings when they announced over the radio, "Don't go out today if you can help it. Your skin, upon exposure, will freeze instantly." They advised you to keep rations in your car, in case it broke down. "Leaving your car to look for help could result in death."

My first winter I was in amazed shock, almost fascinated. My Volkswagen's heating system was like a mosquito bite on an elephant. I frantically bought wool socks, a down jacket, mittens as big as pumpkins. I listened for school closings every morning before I went out—I had landed a job in South Minneapolis, teaching remedial reading, and hoped for a day's reprieve from our iced garage. I was always freezing in the car and holding an ice scraper in my right hand: The car's defrost system was defenseless in this cold.

How did Katagiri end up here in this northern land of Lutherans and Scandinavians? In the mid-sixties, Katagiri was appointed by his Soto Zen sect, from the headquarters in Tokyo, to serve a Japanese-American Zen temple in Los Angeles for two years. From there he went to a similar temple in San Francisco, and then to the San Francisco Zen Center, serving as assistant to the much-loved Suzuki Roshi. The San Francisco Zen community was fueled by the open, idealistic earnest sixties generation. Katagiri was both impressed and dismayed by these free-wheeling, eager American hippies turned Zen students. Zen in Japan had become overly ritualized, bureaucratic, lacking in heart and sincere devotion. It had long since become almost a state religion. Here in America, the students were excited by Zen, full of energy, willing to learn. Katagiri enjoyed their openheartedness. He was young, thirty-five years old. At the beginning, Roshi's wife Tomoe and their young son, Yasuhiko, were still in Japan. He was lonesome for them and the English language did not come easily to him. Yet, I am told, he was full of energy, and taught all the new students how to sit.

Ed Brown, author of *The Tassajara Bread Book* and *Tassajara Cooking* and longtime Zen practitioner, told me that Katagiri taught him how to sit in the early days. Ed came into the Bush

Street zendo with a friend, and after formal sitting, Suzuki asked Katagiri, "Will you please give those two instruction," and Katagiri showed them how to cross their legs and place their hands, how to breathe, and how to hold their heads with chins tucked in.

"While you are sitting, many things will happen," he said, nodding. Long pause and a chuckle. "Don't pay any attention to that. Stay with your breath. Just continue to sit."

One day Suzuki Roshi and Katagiri were in a plane flying from New York to California. Katagiri told me that in the airport in Detroit, where they had to change planes, two businessmen in suits kept staring at them in their black robes. Finally, one of them came over.

"My friend here says you're Korean, but I think you're Japanese. Could you tell us which you are?"

Suzuki looked up and smiled. "We're Americans," he said. Katagiri giggled.

When they were back in the plane, flying over the Iowa corn fields, Suzuki, who was sitting next to the window, motioned for Katagiri to lean over and look out. "This is where the Americans are," Suzuki said, pointing down, and they both nodded.

Katagiri longed to be there, where the Americans were. He longed for the workers to come and practice meditation after work, leaving their lunch pails and shoes by the door, bowing, and sitting zazen. After several years, he was growing tired of the San Francisco hippies. He wanted to teach ordinary people, farmers, mechanics, waitresses, construction workers, how to meditate. After all, he was an immigrant. He, too, had ideas about America.

Only last month, taking a cab in New York City, did I appreciate the vast innocence of a foreigner. My cab driver was from Bangladesh, he told me. I was stunned by the cultural distance he must have traveled to be a taxi driver in Manhattan.

"Where you going?" he asked, when I said I wanted to go to La Guardia.

"To New Mexico," I said.

"Mexico!"

"No, it's a state in the United States, *New* Mexico."

"Oh," he shook his head, "never heard of it." I made the mistake of telling him I was in a bit of a rush. The cab became rubber as it moved between cars in a space big enough for a bicycle. I clutched the back seat. We drove past half-crumbled brick buildings in Harlem.

"It's near Texas," I explained. Not much recognition from him. "Near California," I said.

"Ahh, California. Have you ever been there? I was asked to work there. What's it like? Should I go?"

"What kind of job?"

"I don't know." He shook his head.

"Where in California? It's a big state. It's on the Pacific Ocean. Have you seen it on a map?"

"No."

"Is it near San Francisco?" I asked.

"No, don't think so."

"Near LA?" I quickly corrected myself. "Los Angeles?"

"Yes, yes, I think that's it. Could I drive a cab?"

"I guess so. It's a big city, very spread out. It's summer there all the time."

"No!"

"Yes. It never gets cold."

"No winter?" He shook his head. "No cold. Always hot.

I don't like that." He was quiet a long time. We were in line to pay a toll. He swung into a shorter lane and cut off another yellow cab. The other cab driver screamed out the window.

"Which airline?" he asked. We were nearing the airport.

"American."

We entered the ramp and the cab stopped for me to get out. The driver turned around in his seat. "I thought about it. I'll stay in New York. I don't think I'll move to California."

I nodded. Fate had been sealed that quickly and on so little knowledge.

In 1972, when a small group of Zen students in Minneapolis invited Katagiri Roshi to be their teacher, he jumped at the chance to be in the middle of America and he and his family moved out there.

Stephen Gaskin's commune in Tennessee, called The Farm, heard that a genuine Zen master had just moved to Minneapolis. A bunch of them piled in a bus and drove up. Roshi looked out the window, saw them pull to the curb, and his heart sank. They were outrageous-looking hippies. Though they were not the American workers Roshi dreamed of, it was a good thing they came. There were few Zen students in the Twin Cities. The Farm people joined right in; some became Zen students and helped paint and do construction on the new zendo, which was a rundown house on Lake Calhoun.

When I came to Zen Center in 1978, there were about forty active students. Just forty. And they were mostly from Minnesota. The wild enthusiasm I imagined at the San Francisco Zen Center was not here. Instead the Zen Center took on the qualities of midwestern Minnesota: staid, introverted, grounded, bland, responsible, serious, conservative. I was stunned that there were so few people. In Boulder, the center had at least seven hundred. Because of the cold, people did not follow Katagiri from the West Coast.

If I asked someone at Lama Foundation in New Mexico how they got there, a fantastical story usually ensued: "I walked to the edge of a Himalayan cliff—I'd been in India three years— I was about to jump. I heard a voice, 'Return home. Go to Lama.' I didn't know what Lama was. I trusted God. I wandered. I came to the foot of the mountain in New Mexico."

If I asked Zen students in Minnesota how they got to Zen Center, I heard, "I read a book on Buddhism in religion class and it sounded pretty good, so I came over." Or, "I wanted to learn how to meditate. I heard it was good for you." Nothing fantastical. Ordinary. This was good, but tricky. Zen is about the ordinary, but the vibrant ordinary of things as they are, no illusions, no self-deception, no projections of the self. Midwestern ordinary could appear to be deceptively like Zen ordinary but instead might come out of lethargy, inertia, a deep sleepiness, and have no bite of the unexpected, nothing to hold on to.

Jim White, my poet friend, sat at Zen Center a few times and said, "It's like the Lutheran Church sitting zazen." Still, the students were earnest, serious if not flamboyant, and I was touched by them.

I sat my first seven-day sesshin with Roshi in September, a month or two after I interviewed him. A sesshin is a meditation retreat that begins at five A.M. and continues until nine or later at night. The day's schedule was regulated, with up to fourteen forty-minute sits each day, alternating with ten minutes of walking meditation, a half-hour break after breakfast and dinner, and an hour-and-a-half work period after lunch. Even the meals were eaten in formal oryoki style, which meant in a cross-legged sitting position with three eating bowls in front of you and a highly stylized pattern of mindfulness to serving, meal chanting, eating, and cleaning of the bowls. The entire seven days are done in silence.

During the sesshin, although my brain was racing—like putting a wild boar in a fenced-in backyard—everything actually slowed down. It was as though I was running at two levels— my brain raced while my body was still. I had never before sunk so far into the present moment and connected to the wood floor below me, the slow presence of trees out the window, the natural movement of daylight and its changing shades.

During break after dinner on the first day, I stood out by Lake Calhoun across from Zen Center. I watched black coots swim in and around each other and I watched the dark ripple of lake water. I watched the bikers whiz by on their trek around the lake. I was in another world, but it was in this world. On the second day, I snuck off after dinner to a small grocery, Van's Superette, on the corner of Hennepin and Thirty-fourth, and bought a Kitkat. I mindfully opened the wrapper and chewed the chocolate wafers slowly as I walked back along Thirty-fourth under the tremendous elms.

On the third morning of sesshin, Roshi told us a Zen story. First he made a joke: A Zen master was standing on his balcony in Japan looking out at the birds. Suddenly a swami manifested himself on the balcony. He said proudly, "I traveled here with my psychic powers all the way from India."

The Zen master replied, "What took you so long?"

We all laughed. Roshi laughed, too.

Then he continued the story: The Zen master then said to the swami, "You can keep all your magic. Just leave me the Buddha dharma."

There was a deep silence in the room after this.

Then Roshi continued, "Now do you want me to give an example of Zen magic?" We all nodded.

"There was an old Zen master who lived in a monastery in the mountains. He was taking an afternoon nap. When he woke up, his old disciple, who had been with him for many years, walked in, placed a tray by the bed, and sat down.

"The old roshi looked up. 'Oh, hello,' he said sleepily. 'Let me tell you a dream I just had.'

"The monk disciple said, 'Tell it to me later. Here, have a cup of tea.'"

That was the end of the story. That was Zen magic. That was the Buddha dharma, which meant the essential truth of existence. No dreams. A cup of tea. There was a long silence. Zen stories were like that. They went no place. I'd been up since five A.M. that morning. I was slumped against a back wall under a window: We were supposed to be sitting in an erect position. I started to cry softly to myself. Could things be as simple as that story? Was that allowed in the world? The bell rang. We chanted. Roshi straightened his cushion, bowed, and walked out of the room. We turned, faced the white wall for another forty-minute session of watching our breath.

The last day of that first sesshin, I went to Roshi. "I feel high, like I'm tripping on LSD."

"Pay no attention to that. Continue to feel your breath, bow, drink tea."

When I met my friend Kate the day after, we sat on my porch talking. She said, "Nat, I feel like I'm sitting with a portrait of a woman painted by Picasso. Everything's blown open. Your eye is on your cheek, your lips are on your forehead."

Things changed for me after that sesshin. I went to all the Wednesday night and Saturday morning lectures, though I probably understood only an eighth of what Roshi was talking about.

After one lecture, I visited him in his study and said, "Now that lecture was really boring! I had to do everything to keep awake."

His face fell and I could see he was hurt.

I stopped. "Roshi, you look hurt. How can that be? You're enlightened, you don't have feelings."

But of course he had feelings. He was a human being. I saw that then. I had an erroneous conception of what an enlightened person was like. I'd like to say I had beginner's mind, simple, fresh, innocent, but many times instead I think I was rude, stupid, unfeeling. I butted my head again and again up against what I did not know. I came to him with this ignorance and in exposing it I began to learn the Buddhist teachings. My questions were rooted in my real life, not in some fancy dharma questions I thought I should ask. In a sense, I don't think I'll ever learn so much again, because I'll never be that ignorant again—or naive enough to expose it—and thus will probably not be able to receive so much.

On another occasion, I went to him: "Roshi, I had terrible sex last night. I kept wanting to fall asleep. What should I do?"

Writing these questions now embarrasses me, but it was through them, through his responses, that I began to learn the dharma. I guess you want to know his answer to the sex question. He said, "Practice, make effort." Very simple.

Once after a lecture on the Abhidharma, which is a complicated doctrine on Buddhist psychology, Roshi asked if there were any questions. There was a long silence. I don't think any of us even understood enough about what he was saying to ask a question. All of it was foreign to me; yet, just looking at Roshi, I knew he was saying something I wished I could comprehend. I wished I could rearrange my brain in a moment to match his.

To encourage us, he said again, "Any questions?" Long pause. No response. "Go ahead, you can ask anything, anything you want to know."

I took a breath and raised my hand. He nodded at me. "Roshi, I was wondering, how did you meet your wife Tomoe?" The group laughed.

He smiled and answered me directly. He felt my sincerity. I was trying to get a handle on all this Zen. I started on something elemental: how man meets woman in Japan, how a monk meets someone.

Later, in the basement, some of the older Zen students chastised me for asking that question. They said I was disrespectful.

Tomoe, however, had also been at the lecture. She smiled and said, "Natalie, I never knew the whole story before. From now on, if I want to know something, I'll have you ask Roshi."

There were a lot of women at Zen Center. Some were ordained, and some of these women had shaven their heads. Masculine pronouns were adjusted in the sutras. Gay people came to Zen Center. Roshi watched marriages dissolve and children belong to two households. He watched hundreds of people pass through Zen Center and then never be heard from again. Roshi said, "I can't stop anyone, but I pray for them."

Whether we were there or not, he was there. He sat every morning at five A.M. Once he said, "I'm not here for Minnesota Zen Center. I'm here for all sentient beings every moment forever." This was impressive. Yet it was ordinary. There was no fanfare. He just sat. You sat or didn't sit. There was no comment, no praise or blame. We got no demerits and no stars. This was difficult to get used to. In the first three years I was there, I was always expecting to get yelled at, for Roshi to finally lose all patience with me, grab me by my neck and the seat of my pants and fling me crashing out the window—not the door, it had to be more dramatic, glass had to break, the window frame had to shatter. But he never did throw me out.

Once, though, Roshi did throw someone out. Roy had been there for five years and sat very regularly, but the instant he crossed his legs, he fell into a deep sleep and sometimes even snored. Falling asleep so much is often considered a deep resistance. In all those years, Roshi never said anything to Roy. Then during the last afternoon period of sitting during one day of a sesshin—Roy was in the Buddha hall, an adjunct room to the zendo, fast asleep as usual, and we were all sitting facing the white walls—we heard a huge scream: "Wake up!" Like a flash of lightning I saw out of the corner of my eye—none of us moved, that was zazen, you stayed still under all circumstances—Roshi run into the Buddha hall and lift Roy up. Roy was huge, had been a college football player, I saw him once hold up by himself one whole end of a piano, while Roshi was small, short, maybe five feet three inches, but Roshi hauled him to the back door and threw him out. What I remember most was that scream, "Wake up!" It was clear, with no Japanese accent.

Did Roy wake up? About an hour later he was again sitting in the Buddha hall fast asleep. No one ever said anything about it. We continued in silence for the rest of the week.

Eventually my fear of being thrown out faded away. I was just there. I didn't question any longer whether I belonged or not. I didn't think about it. But many times during dokusan, one-to-one formal interview with the teacher, I moaned to Roshi, "This is no good. I can't sit still; I think all the time—my brain never stops; I hate bowing; and so-and-so makes me so mad." Then I'd pause. "I should leave. I don't belong here."

He nodded. "That's just another thought, that you should leave. Don't be tossed away by it. Continue to sit, to gassho—bow—and drink tea."

Once Ed Brown told me that after a year of being the head cook at the Tassajara Zen monastery, he went to Suzuki Roshi to complain. "So-and-so doesn't cut the carrots right; so-and-so comes late for his shift."

Suzuki sat opposite Ed, nodding and beaming. Ed thought he was commiserating. He went on for ten minutes, recalling every problem, every misdemeanor someone did in the kitchen. Finally, he had nothing else to say; he had emptied himself. He thought Suzuki was going to slap him on the back and say, "I understand, Ed. Good help is hard to find."

Instead, Suzuki was quiet, looked down and then slowly looked at Ed again. "But, you know, Ed, in order to see virtue, you have to have a calm mind."

After I moved to Minneapolis, I was lonesome for the small, intimate writing groups in my living room. They had so much supported my writing life in Taos. Within three months of coming north I volunteered to teach an eight-week workshop as a benefit for Zen Center. I was amazed at how many people signed up. Many were unlikely candidates: four carpenters, an auto mechanic, two cooks, one house cleaner, and several therapists were among the twenty writing students. I had no credentials, yet people were eager to study writing. After the eight-week Zen benefit, which was very successful, I gained the courage to launch two workshops outside the Zen community. I made homemade signs with white paper and a black magic marker: "Eight-week writing group. Cost: $40." I hung the signs at Orr Books at Calhoun Square, in the Uptown area of Minneapolis, and at the local food coops. Within days both workshops were full. I realized that unlike Taos, a city had a large pool of people from which to draw. I spoke to each person on the phone to make sure they weren't dangerous and that I could give them my address and let them into my living room. As I write this now, it seems extraordinarily trusting, but I had no problems. One woman did show up in hair curlers, but that was hardly cause to think I put my life in jeopardy—and she was a good writer, which is what mattered more.

I had great innocent confidence then. I hadn't quite yet formed all my detailed writing rules, but the moment the students arrived, I told them, "We'll do timed writings for ten minutes. Keep your pen moving; don't stop, don't cross out, don't think. Okay, the topic is 'elbows.' Go." And off we went! When the ten minutes were up, we read aloud what we had written. The results were so alive, so dynamic, that no one questioned the process or argued about style or standards or demanded criticism. The classes were as exciting as the ones in Taos, but a bit different. First of all, there were men in these classes. And second, these people were from the Midwest. Their writing stayed in that location. Rarely was there a foreign country mentioned, much less New York, the South, Texas, or California. Actually, California was used, as the example of anything gone wrong, of anything hare-brained, lost, uprooted, unstable, of people gone amok, crazy. A lot was written about grandparents, farms, the weather. These midwesterners were grounded. Writing practice was new to them, but they were smart, knew a good thing, took in everything I said, and practiced hard.

This stuff works, I thought to myself. And not just in Taos. It's real, universal, has a basic sanity that speaks to everyone.

The no-blame-no-praise I learned in Zen penetrated my life and affected my attitude toward writing. More and more I just wrote: no good, no bad. And I encouraged my writing students to write and then just read: no good, no bad. No comment from me or the other students about their writing. After the initial enthusiasm of some of the students in my living room, this non-criticism became unnerving. They had spent so long in public schools that their main model was getting "corrected." They wanted to hear something bad about their piece. In their hearts they knew it was bad, and they wanted me to affirm that fear. When I didn't, there was empty space. That was scary. What was there to hold on to? Nothing. Continue to write, I said.

It was tough, to hold that space of no response as a teacher. I saw how eager everyone was to acknowledge and be acknowledged, even if it was negative. On the few occasions I did say something positive, instead of nothing, they didn't believe me anyway. Sometimes I said after each person read, "Good, good, next person." It allayed or relieved the silence, but I did not mean good as in good versus bad. I meant "good": good to write, good to be alive in a human body and have language, good to be here, all of us sharing this space.

Slowly, slowly like osmosis, this understanding dissolved into me as I practiced zazen with Katagiri Roshi. No good, no bad, just the action: Just pouring tea, just writing, just breathing; just standing, sitting, speaking, or not speaking. This was my Zen education. The process of learning was as deep for me as what I learned, and this I shared with my students, not by talking about it but by allowing empty silent space after someone read, giving them nothing to grab on to, only sitting there with their own breath.

Often Roshi repeated a saying by Dogen, "When you walk in the mist, you get wet." You might not understand everything, but just by being here, you absorb the teachings.

I recited a poem to my perturbed writing students:

> No applause
> No criticism
> Not such a bad
> audience—the apple orchard.

> (John Brandi, *The Crow That Visited*
> *Was Flying Backwards*,
> Tooth of Time Books, 1982)

After our first year in Minneapolis, my husband and I left the Cedar-Riverside area and purchased a duplex with Paul Johnson, an old Zen student. Neil and I lived in the bottom half. It was six blocks from Zen Center. Neil was also practicing, and both of us wanted to be able to walk there. That year I was given the job of Zen host, which meant I took care of all guests and visitors. I was happy to have that job. Paul, with whom we shared the duplex, became doan. He was in charge of the zendo and was there almost every day.

Whenever a guest came, Roshi inevitably asked Paul to take care of that person. When I would see Paul at the house, he'd mention the guest and what he'd done for them.

I became exasperated. Why didn't Roshi send them to me?

After all, wasn't I the host, didn't I have that position? I went and visited him in his study.

"You know, Roshi, you should send people visiting Zen center to me. I'm the host. Don't send them to Paul."

He looked at me, his head to one side. "It's okay to do nothing," he said, and nodded.

Roshi was so ordinary, it was hard to copy him. Usually when we emulate someone we try to take on their qualities. When the Beatles became popular, many people got Beatle haircuts. Trungpa Rinpoche drank a lot, there was a lot of drinking throughout his community.

Roshi's favorite place to eat out was The Embers on Hennepin Avenue. The Embers was a chain restaurant like Denny's. Who in our hip natural-foods, macrobiotic generation wanted to eat there? Once, when my friend Kate and I ate dinner at their apartment above the zendo, Roshi asked us if we wanted wine. Yes, we said. He brought out a gallon box—not even a bottle—of Gallo and put the glasses under the nozzle and out poured some red liquid. Who wanted to copy that? He drank an occasional beer at parties. He ate meat. He had been married for decades. He had two sons who did well in school and he loved to watch TV. He was ordinary with this one difference: He had been a Japanese Zen monk since he was eighteen. For three and a half years, he had studied at Eiheiji, the monastery that is the main training center for Soto Zen, where the ashes of Dogen, that great Zen teacher from the thirteenth century, were kept. He had taken vows to help all beings. He continually told us, "Our goal is to have kind consideration for all sentient beings every moment forever." And when he talked about sentient beings, he included the chair, the pen, the floor, a table.

A friend of mine from Santa Fe went to visit him when she was up in Minnesota.

She said to him, "I'd like to study Zen."

He said, "It's no big deal. Here's a book." He lifted a book off his desk. "You can either fling it down or place it down, like this." He demonstrated placing it down. My friend said the way he placed it, the book became a real being.

"That's all," he said, and smiled.

The tricky thing about Roshi was, the things that were extraordinary about him, you couldn't copy. They came from within him. What you wanted in him had to come from within you. You could get up at four-fifteen A.M. a few times to get to the zendo by five to sit with Roshi because you wanted to be noticed by him or to be with him, but you couldn't keep it up for those reasons, especially since it didn't impress him. Finally, you had to give up all that. You had to do it because it came from inside you, because you wanted to do it, whether he was there or not. And then it even became empty of that. You just did it because you did it.

I had lunch with a friend yesterday at Pasqual's in Santa Fe. Over delicious chili and squash soup, she bemoaned the fact that she couldn't manage to write. I told her she was lazy, that she just had to do it.

She tried to reason as a way to encourage herself. "You mean like I go to the gym regularly to exercise, so I have a healthy body and look good, and I go to twelve-step meetings so I can learn to be a kind person? I manage to do those things regularly. I could go write to—"

"Exercise your brain," I interrupted. I shook my head. "Just do it for no reason. For no purpose." I took another spoonful of soup. "Writing's not gonna save you, help you. I know of no one who has improved as a person because they wrote. They just used up some paper, felled more trees." I paused again, this time to think. "You know, Margaret, you're already a kind person. You go to the twelve-step meetings because you like them." I picked up the water glass. "My body's gonna fall apart whether I exercise or not. You should just write and not think about it so much."

Recently I had some old Zen students to dinner in Taos. Stanley, who is seventy, told us of his first encounter with Zen.

"I was already forty. It was the early sixties in San Francisco. I was a beatnik then, living with a poet. I felt really lost and I think I was probably clinically depressed. I couldn't hold down a job. I had this friend named Susan who was dating this guy named Dan. Susan called me one day and asked me what I thought of Dan.

" 'Well, I hardly know him,' I said. 'Why don't I call him up and get together with him and I'll tell you what I think afterward.'

" 'Okay,' she said.

"So I called Dan, I thought we'd go shoot some baskets or have coffee. He suggested we go meditate with this Japanese man and he'd pick me up early the next morning. Well, I'd never meditated before, but I was game, so I said yes.

"There were five of us there and Suzuki Roshi. It was just at the beginning. No one knew much about Suzuki then. Dan showed me how to sit. I couldn't get my knees down, and through the whole forty minutes I sort of bounced. I don't know what it was."

He demonstrated to us how he sat with his knees up and how he bounced. We laughed.

"When it was over and Dan and I were back in the car, he asked me, 'Well, what did you think of it?'

"I told him, 'Oh, it was okay'—and I knew I'd just found what to do with the rest of my life."

I grew quiet after Stanley told that story. That's how it was in Zen. You'd feel uncomfortable sitting, knees up, you'd bounce, and then know you'd found your life's path. It didn't make logical sense. Something else besides the rational mind was at work. Something quiet, direct, and true, the way being in the presence of a forest feels.

Yesterday I wrote sitting outside at a small card table on the mesa, near my house, facing Taos Mountain. I usually write in cafés, but yesterday morning I wanted to be alone. I spooned cooked oat groats with maple yogurt and a dollop of peach preserves slowly into my mouth. A slight breeze blew across my face and the flies buzzed but didn't bother landing. It took me about an hour to settle into writing that morning and then I enjoyed myself. When I stopped at twelve-thirty, I thought, now this is the life. How could I ever have thought writing was bothersome? (The day before I had once again thought of getting a plumber's permit and giving up being a writer.)

I walked to my car to drive into town. Wild rain clouds suddenly appeared over Taos Mountain. Everything became still. I stopped. I didn't hear flies, distant cars, a plane. Nothing. Then I remembered: Today was the solar eclipse. A man about a quarter of a mile away, standing in front of Kit and Judy's house, was the only other person around. I yelled to him, "Is it happening? What are you doing?"

"I have a device . . ." he yelled back. He was holding something in his hand and beckoning me.

"I don't have time. I've got to get into town," I yelled. It was a quarter to one. I had a lunch date at one. It took at least fifteen minutes to get there.

But this was the famous eclipse! I had heard people were gathering in Mexico and Hawaii, but I hadn't paid much attention. People were making predictions: the end of the world; the beginning. I thought it no more fantastic than the miracle of the sun rising every day. But here it was right now, happening! Spontaneously, the man on the mesa and I ran fast toward each other, jumping over sage bushes. Of course, I had to see the eclipse. He handed me a tin coffee strainer and a piece of paper to put underneath. If I held them the right distance from each other, I could see the moon's shadow blocking out half the sunlight through the holes of the strainer.

"Wow," I said. I looked around. It was still, and way in the distance—fifteen miles away—I could see a ranch house. Usually the sun is too bright, but with the half light, things never seen stepped forward. I didn't know this man. He was visiting next door. We gave each other a big hug. Something great was happening. I ran back to my car and flew into town.

I parked at Doc's. He said he could change my oil while I ate.

Doc's wife said, "You're eating at Lambert's?"

"Yes, it's my favorite," I replied.

"They don't have beans and tortillas," she said in disbelief. She has lived in Taos all her life. Lambert's serves nouvelle cuisine. I went next door. Mirabai was waiting for me. She had studied writing with me when she was twelve years old, back in the seventies, at DaNahazli, the hippie school in Taos. It was when I was just beginning to develop writing practice. We worked together for three years. I remember it was her group that taught me straight honesty. Mirabai had been writing ever since. Now I was treating her to lunch for her thirtieth birthday.

I leaned close after we ordered our food.

"You were at the beginning of the lineage. And you've carried it on. All those kids I taught—you kept going and that's what matters." I paused. "Thank you. It makes me happy." At the time I said this, I had been teaching writing practice for many years, and I had linked it to the long lineage of Zen. Sitting across the table from Mirabai, I felt the space across eighteen years.

The waitress put our plates before us.

"You've already written a novel. We're peers now. Anyone who writes a novel, they've gone beyond teachers. Just keep going, no matter what."

I noticed Nancy Jane, my acupuncturist, in the next room. When the waitress asked if we wanted dessert, I said, "Oh, no," and glanced over to the other room, "but please, Mirabai, get something."

The waitress went down the list: white chocolate ice cream with pecans, strawberry shortcake, lemon tart, chocolate mousse in raspberry sauce—bingo, I thought and kept my opinion to myself—and prune cake. Mirabai said, "I'll have the mousse." Mirabai was a smart person. I was happy.

The waitress brought two spoons and placed the mousse between us. I pushed it over to Mirabai and said, "I'll just taste." I ate more than half, the dark chocolate color intensified by the red sauce intensified by my acupuncturist in the next room. Each time I took a bite, I licked the spoon clean, placed it before me as if I hadn't been using it, and wiped my mouth with the white linen napkin, so if Nancy Jane walked by, it wouldn't look as though I was partaking of dessert. Mirabai shook her head and smiled. I was her old teacher up to my old tricks.

After lunch, I walked to the post office.

The whole day felt huge to me, open, endless, forever. Yet it was ordinary. I eat at Lambert's often. People have thirtieth birthdays. I've had good mornings of writing before. Strange light happens frequently in Taos. Still it was enormous: Mirabai had continued to write from that seed planted when she was twelve years old. I didn't know when I taught back then that anyone would continue—they were all so young—or that I would continue so many years later. We hope for these things, but moment follows moment. Things are unpredictable; lives unfold as days do, and have their own composition.

It was enormous for me to have found Katagiri Roshi in that cold northern state, but the daily life of sweeping the zendo floor, lighting incense, walking to the zendo to meditate was ordinary, sometimes boring, and sometimes I wondered what I was doing there, what I was doing with my life. Yet our lives are big. We may decide to become an engineer and end up a poet.

I know even Roshi sometimes questioned what he was doing in Minnesota with these conservative students. Once in a lecture he told us, "During the last sesshin, while we were sitting, I found myself thinking, 'Is this all I'm going to do with my life: just sit?' Then I caught it. Another thought." He showed us how he waved the thought away with his hand and laughed.

But through his Zen practice, he had a way to understand

his life. Not wanting to sit was just another thought. He did not get tossed away by it.

Recently, I sat a sesshin with Sekkei Harada Roshi, from Hoshinji, a monastery in Japan. He is considered a great Zen teacher, and this was his first visit to America. Someone asked him, "Even though judging mind is troublesome, we still have to discriminate—choose a job, a partner, a place to live. How should we do this?"

Harada nodded. He said, "Yes, I, too, am a man of many delusions. For instance, several times a year I have to travel to Tokyo. You can get there from the monastery either by plane or train. Sometimes even to the last minute I cannot decide which to take." There was a pause. Then he added, "But I am not perplexed by it."

Suzuki Roshi once said about questioning our life, our purpose, "It's like putting a horse on top of a horse and then climbing on and trying to ride. Riding a horse by itself is hard enough. Why add another horse? Then it's impossible." We add that extra horse when we constantly question ourselves rather than just live out our lives, and be who we are at every moment.

My marriage was somehow slowly disintegrating after two years of being in Minnesota. Our time was probably up after we left Taos, but the love was strong, and it lingered and carried me to Minnesota, where I met my Zen teacher. Our education doesn't prepare us for this continuous coming together and parting. Instead of letting go after Taos, Neil and I married and I thought marriage would last forever. I would be safe. I would get to keep our love. My mother and society told me it was forever and I wanted to believe it, though divorce was all around me. I continued to practice Zen, deepen my writing, and battle my husband. Our lives were turning. We had different destinies, different needs—it was too hard to carry our old hippie lives from Taos into the hazards of the city—and neither of us wanted to face it, so we fought instead, tried to get the other to do what we wanted.

I went to Roshi about it. "Roshi, he makes me so mad. What should I do?"

"You have already let him know what you want. Now keep quiet. Take care of your life, take care of your writing, take care of Neil's life and," he paused, "hopefully he'll see into your heart." He laughed. "If he's not too ignorant."

"What should I do?" I scrunched up my face. It was inconceivable what Roshi said. Keep quiet? I was furious and heated up a lot of the time.

"You want me to tell you again?" he asked.

Yes, I nodded.

"Okay, take care of your life, take care of your writing, take care of his life, and be quiet," he said.

I was incredulous. "What should I do?" I asked again.

"You want me to tell you straight?"

"Yes," I said.

"Keep your mouth shut," he directed me.

I was stung, insulted. I left quickly and refused to visit him for quite a while. I'd never heard of such a thing. I was mad, why should I shut up? Several months later, I realized Roshi gave me the only advice that would have worked, but I was too angry at the time to be able to understand it, much less carry it out. The only thing I knew to do when there was trouble was to dive in. To step back was inconceivable. And I realized he never said *not* to say how I felt. I needed to say it, then be quiet.

But instead, Neil and I kept fighting. In one dramatic moment, I yanked the wedding ring off my finger, flung it into the toilet, and then flushed. Both Neil and I stood over the bowl, aghast, watching the water swirl, disappear and then rise again calmly—without my gold wedding band. Another time, I threw a beautiful chocolate birthday cake I'd made for Neil face down on the linoleum floor. My emotions and his were all out, raging, unbridled will against will. We crashed through our marriage. What Roshi asked, "Keep your mouth shut," or just being quiet, was impossible for me then. I could not be quiet; I was a wild bull. I had no refinement, care, mindfulness, or understanding.

I understood Roshi's advice too late. Four months after that meeting with Roshi, Neil and I separated. The pain of separation sobered me.

It was only then I realized that if I went to Roshi for advice, I had to follow it—whether I immediately understood it or not—for at least six months. He had something of value to say. Otherwise, why go to him? His advice about my marriage had been wise. I couldn't hear it when he gave it, but later I carried it within me.

I'd begun to trust in his way. He came from such a different angle than I had ever known. But slowly, slowly, I was learning that angle, learning through the suffering in my life, and through time, experience, mistakes, coming up against him, running away, coming back.

Roshi told me that he was lonely as a Zen master, but that he didn't let the loneliness toss him away, it was just loneliness. I realized that I was growing used to the loneliness of being a writer. It came with the trade. I no longer ran from it, but the loneliness of being separated from Neil was another matter. I'd come home at night after teaching poetry in a public school and sit down on the couch. I'd just sit there. There was only me. The empty house stunned me. Now I had two lonelinesses—of work and of love. I'd always lived in communes and communities before I met Neil, so I thought I'd do that again.

"You need to be alone," Roshi told me. "It is the terminal abode. You can't go any deeper in your spiritual practice if you run from loneliness."

I listened to what he said. I remained in the lower half of our duplex on Emerson Avenue, while Neil lived several blocks away in an efficiency apartment.

I moved deeper into Zen and writing. They were mine alone, and the loneliness I felt was a dark background in this northern city where I always felt a foreigner. That loneliness pushed me deeper. I wanted to find a way out.

In one lecture, Roshi told us a koan from the *Mumonkan* or *Gateless Gate:*

One day a big congregation of monks had been arguing about Buddha nature. When Nansen heard them, he held a cat up in front of them.

"Does this cat have Buddha nature?" Nansen asked.

No one answered, so Nansen cut the cat in half.

That evening, Joshu returned and Nansen told him what had happened. Joshu put his sandals on his head and walked out.

Nansen said, "If you had been here, you could have saved the cat."

I had heard this before. I always got stuck on the sandals.

Then Roshi began talking about the pickles he ate in the monastery after the war. Everyone was very poor. Often they were served hot water with three grains of rice floating on top and those pickles—"We had to eat them silently." He turned to us, "Can you chew a pickle silently?" He made a face and imitated eating a pickle silently.

Well, I'm not sure, I'd think to myself.

At this point, if you were a new visitor you'd be laughing as I had when I first came to Zen Center. Eat a pickle silently? You'd think this Zen master was very funny and he was, but the Zen students did not laugh; we were odd, serious, poker-faced. The visitor might comment later how dead the Zen students seemed.

Mostly the visitor never returned, but the students continued to come. What the visitor experienced in the Zen students was their basic human resistance. We had passed the stage of enthusiasm; we were coming up with our defenses, our resistances. Often as I listened, I projected my feelings onto Roshi and thought, he's boring, he's not clear, Zen is dumb. But something in me didn't quite believe it. I still wanted to know whether the cat had Buddha nature.

Last January I taught a week-long writing workshop in Taos for people who had studied with me before. After Tuesday morning's class I thought to myself, these people hate me. I know them and they hate me and they hate writing too. Why did they come? They've been here before. They know what it's like.

Then I remembered the zendo. The love affair with writing was over. They were taking it more seriously. All their resistances had come up. That afternoon I explained it to them: "Last year, when you came it was all new. Writing practice was a joy. You discovered you could write, you recovered old memories. This year you want writing more, you have expectations, you suffer. It's okay, just keep doing it. You're meeting more of yourself."

They felt a bit relieved, but not much. Resistances are painful, and they deepen as we deepen.

Roshi said, "Nansen didn't need to cut the cat in half. In Soto Zen you don't cut the cat, but Rinzai is very swift." He motioned with his hand cutting off his head, showing the way he imagined Rinzai to be. Soto and Rinzai are two different sects of Zen. Katagiri was a Soto Zen master. He laughed. "Soto is different," he said. "It's like the not-too-bright, kindly older uncle." He liked that image. He laughed and laughed. I tried to grunt up a half smile. My knees hurt. It was nine-thirty on a Wednesday night, bitter cold outside. Someone over in China centuries ago was cutting up cats in the zendo. This is a weird religion, I thought. Mostly I never called it a religion. That word made me nervous. Zen was just something I got caught up in, and I was somehow trusting this little Japanese man in a way I had never trusted anyone. He wanted nothing from me and spoke to me from the bottom of the earth, at least from the bottom of his mind with no distortions.

Minds, my mind and yours, are run by the same principles. We are not unique. We mirror what is around us. If we walk into a red room, we become red. If we are always in a group of angry people, it is hard not to become angry. If we are with someone who is clear, our mind reflects that back and we become clearer. Roshi gave me a vision of a different kind of mind.

After the first sesshin we sat together, Neil said to me in amazement, "Nat, he knows his own mind. He knows what he thinks. How many people can you say that of?"

One spring, the sangha, the Zen Center spiritual community, decided we had to reach out to the Twin Cities community in the hope of receiving some big donations. Minnesota Zen Center was not good at raising money. We had our yearly summer rummage sales, where I had my spontaneous poetry booth, and we baked breads that people bought after lecture on Saturdays, but we decided that not enough people knew about us. We would have a lovely Sunday afternoon tea and invite guests who could potentially contribute large sums to our waning funds. We set up card tables in the zendo—we didn't want our guests to have to sit on the floor with their legs crossed as we did. We wanted them to be comfortable, and we rented lovely white linen tablecloths. We baked small square tea cakes and thin butter cookies. We served tea from beautiful rented silver tea servers. We wanted people to feel the elegance of Zen. We wanted them to like us.

Prestigious people came: lawyers, university administrators, a journalist, even the owner of a downtown department store. There were about thirty-five people in all. After a time of tea and cookies, cordial conversation, we asked Roshi to come down and give us a lovely Zen talk—maybe he'd talk about generosity, about being in the moment, or something Americans are wild about from the movies: the samurai. Roshi was ideal for a fund-raiser. With his erect posture, his beaming, alive face, he was just what you'd envision a Zen master should look like.

Roshi came down the stairs in his black robes, stood in front of the group seated at the tables, bowed, smiled, nodded, and then began.

"You know, all of you are going to die someday."

No, Roshi, no, we thought, and the visitors drinking their tea out of lovely white tea cups stopped their cups in midair, before they got to their mouths, the steam from the hot water covering their faces.

Roshi went on. It was one of his long talks, punctuated

often by our impermanence and imminent death. As soon as it was over, people bolted for the door. Not a dime was put into the donation box.

Please understand that Roshi did not give this talk to be mean or sarcastic or rebellious. He spoke evenly, kindly. The morning before, he had lectured on this very subject and he was merely continuing the conversation. It would never have occurred to him to adjust a talk to please people or not to tell the truth of his mind. He said to me often, "I'm sorry for you. I do not give you a piece of candy." I do not give you what you'd like, what would please you, but would not be true. I do not feed your illusions.

Once I checked with him before I asked him something, "No candy?"

"No candy," he said and shook his head.

I was pleased. I trusted him. I knew he'd give me an answer I didn't usually understand, but I'd chew on it for a long time until I tasted its noncandy flavor.

I was absorbing Roshi's mind, trying to fathom where he came from. I knew it was a big place, the biggest I'd ever seen. I wanted that largeness for myself; mostly I thought that immense mind might be impossible to attain, but I continued anyway.

A beginning writer loves an author and studies her until she has absorbed that author's style and moves and ways, until she realizes that what she loves is also in herself and that she, too, has the possibility of being a Toni Morrison, a Rita Mae Brown, a Carson McCullers. This is one of the best ways to learn writing.

In this same way, I was digesting Roshi's mind, the mind of no-self, of the Zen present moment, of wisdom and compassion, detail, care, and humor. He became my Great Teacher, yes, and also my Great Writing Teacher. It was through him I understood the mind, and the mind after all is the territory all writers must journey through.

At the end of his lecture on Nansen and the cat, Roshi turned to us. "Do you understand what I mean?"

We nodded.

He shook his head. "No, you don't," then he made a face, "and it's not because of my Japanese accent." He paused and his face lit up. "I'll give you a hint," he said. "If you want to find Buddha nature, love someone and care for them."

Every fall and spring Zen Center offered a hundred-day training period, which meant being at the zendo every morning except Sunday at four-thirty A.M. The students who signed up took turns each morning to talk from four-thirty to five on a given topic. Then we sat for two periods, chanted, cleaned the zendo and left by eight A.M. to go to our jobs in the world. We returned at seven P.M. for two sitting periods before we went home to sleep. The training also required being at the zendo every Saturday, all day, sitting a weekend sesshin once a month, and at least one seven-day sesshin during the hundred days.

After being at Zen Center a year and a half, I signed up for a training period in the fall. Getting up at four A.M. every morning to get to the zendo by half past was one of the hardest things I'd ever done and one of the most secretive, deep, wild, and scary. I'd rarely wakened at four except to turn over and go back to sleep. And there I was doing it every day. I found a pocket of darkness I'd never known before and it felt like it was all mine. The people in the houses I walked past were all asleep and there was rarely a car on the street. The traffic signal blinked red, then green, then yellow for no one. Down the alleys I'd grown to love, behind people's houses along their backyards, I'd walk on solid ice in weather well below zero as we moved into late November and December and I was wrapped in more and more clothes against the wind chill that was no longer just the news announcer's term; I was experiencing it with everything in me. During that training period, I entered another part of my life, something that was always there, but usually I was asleep when it was happening. Now I and fourteen other Zen students carried our unconscious minds still raw from having wakened in the middle of our dreams and sat on black zafus in a white-walled room lit by a candle, the smoke of incense wafting by, watching our minds and feeling our breath. At the time I was not attuned to the wonder. I was mostly tired.

I went to Roshi: "Roshi, I'm exhausted. I need to sleep."

"Oh, you don't need sleep. If you're tired, just take a little catnap at the bus stop, while you're waiting for the bus."

"Um, hum," I said and yawned.

At the time I was resident poet at Andersen elementary school. A newspaper photographer came in one day to snap pictures of our class. One photo was in a neighborhood newspaper the next week. You can see me droopy-eyed in front of the class. The funny thing was that while my body was sleepy, I had tremendous energy and vigor.

One girl in a sixth-grade class I was teaching—her name was Tonya, black, bright, sassy—said out loud to the girl next to her so everyone could hear, "You know, I been thinking lately. Natalie looks like one of them people I see on TV. You know, they cross their legs and close their eyes. Suppose to be peaceful." She scrutinized me up and down. "Know what I mean?"

I was copying on the board the poem, "The White Horse," by D. H. Lawrence, and I turned in the middle of the last line. I gave Tonya a big smile. "You're smart. How did you know?"

"I just did," she said, pleased. "Show us."

I turned to the rest of the class. "Do you know what she's talking about? It's called meditation." With one sweep of my hand, I pushed aside everything on the teacher's desk and hopped up. "Here." I crossed my legs, put my hands on my knees, straightened my back, and told them, "When I close my eyes, I'm going to feel the breath going in and out at my nose." I closed my eyes and felt my breath for three inhales and three exhales. The kids were mesmerized by my stillness, as though feeling one's breath was the most magical thing.

"Do you want to try?" I asked.

They nodded cautiously. They all sat at their wooden desks, I explained how to meditate in a chair, and at two-thirty in the afternoon in a Minneapolis public school they felt their breath.

When we all opened our eyes again, I said quietly, "Amazing, huh?"

Some nodded tentatively. Just then, the classroom teacher walked in. She abruptly stopped at the door. I was on her desk.

"Oh." I smiled. "I am teaching them the measure of a poetic line."

"Uh-huh." She nodded and turned abruptly to leave.

Sitting on her desk top, I put my palms together and bowed to her back going through the doorway and then I turned and bowed to my wonderful breathing students sitting all in rows before me.

That first training period was hard. It broke me, because I wanted to do everything in my regular life—go to my teaching job,

write poetry, meet friends for dinner, go to movies, go dancing
with Neil (we were still together then)—*and* do training period.
Usually, I managed to do whatever I wanted. Training period
taught me I was limited: I had a human body. I had to make
choices. I struggled a lot with this. I remember one Saturday
night falling asleep on the floor at a party Kate was having.

I came face to face with my profound rebelliousness. I
wanted to do what I wanted to do. I went into the Zen kitchen
right after a lecture about mindfulness in taking care of our
cups and spoons so as not to pass around winter colds and flu.
I walked up to a big jar on the shelf, opened it, stuck my finger
in over and over, and put big gobs of peanut butter in my mouth
as I stood by the back door in full sight, just as all the Zen
students were leaving for the night.

Training period ended on a cold Saturday. That night we
had a poetry reading in the zendo and a lot of my non-Zen
poet friends came. As a Zen student, I was supposed to wear
black or at least quiet colors. That night I wore a bright red
skirt and a purple sweater. When the reading was over, a bunch
of us were headed out to a bar. I was very happy. Training
period was over; I didn't have to go back to Zen Center and
sit in the early morning for months if I didn't want to; though
I knew Monday morning Roshi would be there, training period
or no training period.

About to leave the zendo, I was standing by the steps that
led up to Roshi's apartment with my poet friends surrounding
me. Roshi was walking toward the stairs. I waved to him gaily,
"Bye, Roshi, you won't see me for a while."

He stopped, looked straight at me. "I'm sorry for you,"
he said.

Everything stopped for me in that moment. I don't think
my friends even noticed the interchange. I didn't care if they

did. He didn't say it to shame me. He handed me the truth. It was an even statement. He was telling me you can't pop out of your life, run from who you are. I had the illusion that if I didn't come to sit, I was getting away from something. I heard what Roshi said and understood what he meant. I never forgot it, but I wasn't ready to receive it just then. My rebellion was too deep; my lack of surrender too apparent; though what was I rebelling against but myself? At Zen Center I could come and go as I pleased.

A year and a half later I wanted to do another training period. By then I had digested what had happened the last time. I saw that I had to make choices; I couldn't do everything. Plus I was in the middle of a divorce. Neil and I had already separated our stuff. He got the kitchen table; I got the rocker. We both wanted the couch; I took the dining room table instead. There was a resignation now, a painful quiet. I was slowed down, sad. I resolved to give this training period my full attention, broken only by my work.

However, just before I signed up, I heard from someone that a year earlier Scott Edelstein had wanted to sign up for a training period but he couldn't attend the Monday night lecture, which was only for training period students. He had to teach a class on Monday nights. Roshi told him to forget it if he couldn't come Monday nights, that the lecture was important, that he should sign up another time.

Coincidentally, I had to teach writing on Monday nights of the training period I wanted to sign up for. It was at a community college, and I had signed a contract to do it several months before. I didn't think it would be a problem until I heard about Scott. I decided to go to Roshi and explain my situation. I was sure I could talk him into letting me sign up. It was a ridiculous idea, the idea of trying to talk him into something. His grounding was different from mine. I went trying to defend, argue. He was defenseless, still. His grounding was groundless. I went with a sword and when I put it through him I found there was nothing there, nothing to fight. Each time I was startled, but did that stop me? No. The next time I went to him for something I would rev up for a fight.

Here I was again, this time trying to persuade him to let me sit training period and be absent on Monday nights, because of my teaching commitment. I'd tell him I'd have another Zen student take copious notes on Monday night; I'd listen to the taped lecture immediately on Tuesday morning, I'd . . . I'd . . . I can't remember now all the angles I figured, but I do remember walking over to Zen Center one morning at the end of August, down the tree-lined street full of September marigolds and petunias, going over my tactics in my mind to make sure I had included everything, that I couldn't imagine one place where Roshi could catch me. I was determined this time that he would not surprise or shock me.

He was sitting behind his low desk on a cushion. I'd made an appointment earlier. I walked in. I sat down on a zafu and faced him across the desk.

I began: "I want to sit training period. You told Scott . . ." I began the recitation of all my carefully planned tactics. After I had completed only a sentence or two, he turned and looked out the window. I felt ridiculous. I was talking to the side of his face. He'd never done this to me before. I rattled on until I was finished. I didn't know what else to do.

When I was done, he turned to me: "What do you want?"

"I want to sit this fall's training period, but I have to teach Monday nights and I can't come to lecture," I said.

"I'll lecture on Tuesday nights," he said.

"You can't do that!" I was startled.

"Why not? You said you can't come on Mondays, can you?"

"No," I shook my head.

He opened his calendar book. "Yes, I can do Tuesdays."

"But, Roshi," I was getting a little hysterical, "training period lecture is *always* on Monday nights. For years! You can't change it."

"Well, you can't come Monday night and I can do Tuesday."

I was discombobulated. I wanted to say, but what about a year ago with Scott, what about you being the Zen master and me just a dumb student, aren't you more important, what about all the years we've done it one way?

"Anything else?" he asked.

"No." I didn't move. I blinked a few times. "Thank you."

He smiled.

I left. I remember going down those carpeted stairs in my bare feet. A big lake had opened in me where before normal things like a stomach, kidneys, spleen used to hang out. The man was empty; Roshi was empty. He came from no angle. Not better or worse than I, not Zen master. From no time, no way it was done in the past dictating the present. At that moment, he came from nothing. No identity. No hierarchy. No schedule. He certainly didn't come from a story a year ago about Scott Edelstein.

Everyone of my generation in those days was trying to find a center. Roshi didn't have a center. There was no self. He didn't exist in any way I usually understood my world. I'd known good people—my grandmother, Mr. Clemente—but this was different. I was profoundly moved and quiet. There wasn't anything my brain could grab on to.

When training period did begin a month and a half later, lecture was on Monday night. Nothing was ever said or explained to me. Maybe a bunch of Zen students who had already signed up protested the switch from Monday to Tuesday. I doubt it. I taught my Monday night writing group. Roshi lectured that night. I didn't hear his lectures on tape or check with another student. It didn't matter. I woke at four A.M., and I went to the zendo. I went in the evenings, on weekends.

In January, I saw him about something else. "You did pretty good," he nodded. He meant training period.

I smiled.

When Thich Nhat Hanh, a Vietnamese Buddhist monk, came over to this country to advocate a cease-fire in Vietnam, people who heard him speak asked, "Are you from the north?"

"No," he said.

"Are you from the south?" they asked.

"No," he said. "I'm from the center."

It felt as though Roshi came from a bigger place than over here or over there. The important thing about being around him was that I saw between the cracks; I saw him when he wasn't lecturing or sitting, officially being roshi. What amazed me was there was no difference in him. I'd known writers who were exquisite, deep, tender human beings on the page and monsters in person, rude, arrogant, alcoholic, undependable. There was a huge gap between what they wrote and who they were. I experienced Roshi as a whole, gapless.

I remember one Saturday afternoon I was sweeping in the kitchen. It was late March, gray, a bit windy, always cold, but bearable now, winter's back had been broken. You could stand outside and your face wouldn't freeze off. The phone rang. It was Pam. She was already twenty minutes late to pick up Roshi to drive him to the airport. She called to say she'd be another ten minutes.

Oh, my god, I thought. He'll miss his plane. I frantically went looking for him.

He was standing outside by the curb next to a valise. It was not a suitcase, modern with zippers and nylon. It was a valise, square, gold colored, with latches. Roshi just stood there in his black robes as though he had no idea Pam was late. He stood, not waiting, not impatient, just standing.

I ran to him. "Roshi," I called. "Pam will be another ten minutes." My hands were thrown up in the air. I was probably shrieking.

He nodded, unperturbed. "Thank you," and just continued to stand. He wasn't waiting; he wasn't coming; he wasn't going.

I walked back up the walkway, broom in hand. Several times I looked back over my shoulder. He was still standing there, a green army jacket over his black priest robes. That presence, that being present, stunned me. My whole body relaxed. It seemed much more important than making the plane. Pam was going to get there when she got there. Meanwhile, he was standing. I became quiet as I returned to sweep the kitchen.

Until I saw that kind of equanimity I didn't know it was possible. Nothing before in my American world had expressed it. I remember thinking, it's actually okay not to get frantic, to allow things to be. I'd scrunch up my face. Naa, I'd say, the world can't run that way—he's an anomaly. But I wanted to be around it. My whole heart yearned for it. I was seeing something I couldn't express, that actually wasn't very interesting to talk about. I'd try to explain:

"Well, I saw him standing outside," I'd tell a friend.

"Yeah?" my friend would reply.

"He was standing," I'd say.

"What was he doing while he was standing?"

"Nothing."

"Nothing?" My friend would scratch his ear. "So?"

"Like so," I'd try to stand as Roshi stood.

"So what?" My friend would ask.

I didn't know "what." I just went over to Zen Center. It wasn't explainable, in the same way writing wasn't explainable. I learned more about writing from watching his feet, or the way he bowed, than I could from any poetry workshop.

Gary Snyder wrote:

Meditation looks inward, poetry holds forth. One is private, the other is out in the world. One enters the moment, the other shares it.... The one goes back to essential moments of stillness and deep inwardness, and the other to the fundamental impulse of expression and presentation.

(Introduction to *Beneath a Single Moon*, Shambhala, 1991)

It seemed to me that in order to "share" the moment in the writing of poetry, one had to experience it, know it, be in it. Being around Roshi, I got a taste of what a moment might be and how one might be in it. From there, my impulse to express it came naturally, but without Zen, without being present, my foundation for writing was shaky. Without some foundation, my writing was full of thought on thought; nothing down to earth; I was piling sand on sand. Finally, what was I talking about anyway?

I recently attended a one-day mindfulness retreat at my friend Cynthia's, in Santa Fe. All day we had been doing sitting and walking meditations, eating, gardening, all mindfully, all with attention. At the end of the day, still sitting, we passed around tea and cookies and each person spoke whatever was on his or her mind. There were seven or eight of us. I listened to people speak. I blinked my eyes. My mind was quiet. I honestly had no thought, nothing to say, but it was time to share, to be a part of the community.

When it was my turn, suddenly a haiku I'd read many times in class when I taught workshops came floating up through my mind. I saw it and recited it.

> Simply I'm here
> Simply snow falls.

Then I turned to Cynthia. I looked at Naomi across from me. "I have no idea who wrote it. Shiki, maybe Shiki did." My brain was not functioning. Just as I said "Shiki" for the second time, black space opened in front of me and out of it was thrown up the word "Issa."

"Issa! Issa. It was Issa who wrote it!" I said, flushed and excited, and I interrupted the person next to me, who was about to speak.

Usually, it's no big deal to say something, remember something else, and correct yourself, but what was so exhilarating for me was that I actually watched each thought arise. When I saw "Issa," it felt as though the black chasm of time and space had opened up and Issa himself in a fit of indignation at his haiku being misrepresented had flung out his name through five hundred years, and it echoed, shimmering in front of me at the very top edge of its flight where it arrived in that living room late that May afternoon and I grabbed it and called it out.

Staying at that level of thought formation—where one can

actually watch the thoughts arise——is very invigorating and vital, and the impulse from that level is a true place to write from. It is fundamental expression coming out of fundamental stillness. That is why I tell my students, "When you do writing practice, sometimes you get high, feel happy and whole for the rest of the day, and you don't know why. It is because you contacted first thoughts, before they became fettered with second and third thoughts. You stayed with the real grit of your mind."

After four years at Zen Center, during a seven-day sesshin, I went to Roshi. "You know, the more I sit, the more Jewish I'm feeling."

"That makes sense," he said. "The more you sit, the more you become who you are."

This feeling of being Jewish deepened in me. I wanted to know what it meant to be Jewish. Though my family was culturally Jewish——there were smatterings of Yiddish spoken by my parents and grandparents, we ate chicken soup and gefilte fish, felt the shadow of the concentration camps, lit Hanukkah candles——there was nothing spiritual or religious about our home. My father had been brought up religiously and he rebelled. When he was thirteen and had to change in the locker room for gym, his classmates made fun of the prayer shawl he wore under his undershirt. That night, he told me, he went home and told his mother, "No more. I'm not wearing it." And at sixteen when he got his driver's license, he snuck into the family's navy blue Ford and drove it down the street on Yom Kippur, the highest holy day, when you are only allowed to walk. "I crashed the car," he told me. "God was warning me, but, otherwise, that religious stuff is a lot of malarkey." This was my religious instruction from my father. Later, as an adult, I heard that my great-grandfather on my father's side was a holy man, that he wandered from family to family teaching Hebrew and the Torah at heder, Jewish school, that he had no home of his own.

On my mother's side of the family, my grandfather often repeated, "It's so good to be in America. You don't know how good you have it." He'd come over from Russia when he was seventeen to avoid the draft there. He'd seen Cossacks ride through his small shtetl and kill people. When he arrived in the United States, he threw off Judaism as archaic. He wanted to be an American. The day before Yom Kippur, he and my grand-mother parked their car several blocks from their apartment in Brooklyn, and in the morning, when all Jewish families dressed up and walked to shul, to the synagogue, my grandfather and grandmother and their three children dressed up, too. They walked like the other families, but not to shul, to the car, got in, out of sight of their neighbors, and drove out to Long Island for a picnic. When I asked my mother once, "What is God?" she said, "It is goodness. Wherever you see good, you see God." That was a good answer. It satisfied me.

Now, twenty-two years later, Judaism haunted me in the zendo. What was it? And what was this foreign religion, Zen, that I was practicing, when I had turned my back on something that was rightfully mine? There were no interfaith marriages in my family. I was one hundred percent Jewish—no mixed blood. What did that mean? Perhaps I had been arrogant. I had turned my back on my own religion and was studying something foreign.

I went to Roshi. "I'm going to study Judaism. I don't know what it is. I'm going to leave Zen Center for a while."

He nodded. "Remember, whatever you do, the one true test of a religion. Ancestors, history doesn't matter—what mat-ters is that it can help you here and now in your life."

I was naive. I'd never gone to temple, never met a rabbi, except Zalman Schacter, and that was at Lama Foundation, not in a synagogue. I called several in the Twin Cities and asked them to meet me for lunch. I thought rabbis would be like Roshi. Roshi was my archetype for someone spiritual.

The rabbis I met—all men—one from a reform synagogue, one from a conservative orientation, another from the Lubovich organization, were friendly, warm, opinionated, distracted, talkative. With one especially, I wanted to say, "Please, slow down, connect with your breath." None had the presence of Katagiri. Each one at some point in the conversation bent close to me. "Zen, Buddhism, it's not as deep, big as Judaism. It's okay, but it's not the same."

I was surprised. "Do you know much about Zen? Have you sat?"

"I don't need that. I've read a little," the conservative rabbi said.

We went on to talk of Minneapolis, intermarriage, education.

This couldn't be. Where was a person like Roshi in all this? I took some classes on Judaism; I went to services; I studied Hebrew. In Hebrew class, we had an Israeli instructor named Tuvia. He presumed we all pretty much knew Hebrew; after all, it was his native language. I knew nothing, not even the alphabet, but I loved the class. I constantly nudged Carol, the woman in front of me, to give me the answers. She was a dermatologist, brought up on a North Dakota farm, who planned to convert. At the beginning of the course, we all chose a Hebrew name. I chose Malka, which means "queen." I liked playing at a new identity, an ancient Hebrew one.

After taking the Hebrew class for two quarters, I won a Bush Fellowship in poetry and with the money I went to Israel for three months. In Jerusalem, I went to Sabbath dinner at the homes of different Hasidic families. One Hasidic sect had a movement to bring wayward Jews back to the fold. I went often because the Hasids felt closest to what I knew of religion.

At one Sabbath in the Old City, I asked the head of the family over dinner, "What practice is there that I can do every day?"

"Get married and have children," he told me. There were thirteen of his children at the table.

I liked this man; I liked his family. They liked me. It was obvious I was a religious person; I accepted and appreciated their Hasidic tradition.

"Yes, but I'm not married. I don't have children. What can I do?" I asked again.

It seemed obvious to him. "Get married and have children."

I walked home that night through the streets of Jerusalem, past Hasidic Jews in fur hats gathering in front of a small synagogue, the air smoky under street lights. I felt I was back many centuries. I passed rose vines climbing up Jerusalem pines, down cobblestone streets and houses built of pink Jerusalem stone. This was ancient and beautiful, but I could not find a way in. I was a modern woman, a feminist, a writer, an American. I wanted a practice, and so far I had discovered it only in the Eastern world.

I envied my parents when they visited me in Jerusalem. They seemed comfortable there, at home. They spoke Yiddish, the language they had learned in their Brooklyn homes, with people they met on the streets. One Israeli man came up to my father on Rehov Jaffa, tapped him on the stomach, said something, and then walked arm and arm with him for a block. My mother and I trailed behind. When we came to the corner, the Israeli waved good-bye.

I turned to my father. "What did he say to you? Did you know him?"

"Naa," my father shook his head. "We spoke Yiddish. He said I should lose some weight. Did you notice how trim all the men are here? It must be because of the army. I told him I was American. He said he knew."

"How do you feel so comfortable here?" I had struggled for three months to feel at all relaxed. There were Jews here, my people, but it was also a foreign country.

"Oh," my father waved his arm, "it's just like old Brooklyn."

My parents had a natural Jewish identity from being brought up in a Jewish neighborhood. They took it for granted. They never felt the need to pass it on. I was brought up in suburban Long Island, many times the only Jew in my class. I had no such strong identity. Suburbia had neutralized my roots, washed them away.

When I returned from Jerusalem, I went to Roshi. "Roshi, I think it's driving me nuts. It's like an ornate tapestry. I can't find a way in. I get lost in the history, the holocaust. Judaism seems sexist, opinionated."

He shook his head. "Pay no attention to that. Stand up with what you have learned here and continue to penetrate. When you get to the heart of Judaism, you'll find Zen."

I took a deep breath, nodded, and left.

One late afternoon in early October at a Yom Kippur service in a synagogue on Dupont Avenue, five blocks from the zendo—I'd been fasting all day and had walked early that morning through fallen brown leaves—I touched it, touched something. I held the prayer book in my hand, "Let there be grace and kindness, compassion and love," we recited—a moment when everything opened. There among my Jewish brothers and

sisters, I felt that deep stillness, that quiet, that golden joy I felt
in the zendo during sesshin—it was everywhere.

After that I could return to Zen Center, knowing that yes,
where I came from, the religion of my ancestors had it, too.
There was no barrier in me: Zen versus Judaism. It was everywhere. There was a peace in me after that. I did not need to
turn my back on anything.

Neil and I were divorced now. He had moved to the West
Coast six months earlier and I was in the deep north on my
own. Everything I looked at seemed to be dying. Something
was dying in me and that sorrow slowed me down. Slowed
down, I saw things more: the sparrows on the fire escape of a
brick building, corn stalks dry in the November wind, the moon
over the Mendota Bridge, long shadows at noon because the
sun was so far south. I saw a broken man, a Chippewa down
from the reservation, on the corner of First Avenue early one
morning, the breath of cars and buildings coming out in blasts
of blue smoke against the steel cold air. He had only one glove
on and that one was torn. I stood and looked at him. I pulled
off my wool mittens and walked to the corner. "Here," I said
and stretched out my bare hand that held them.

His movements were jerky, hesitant. He took the limp
gloves. He nodded. I nodded. There was a scar under his right
eye. He wore a green army jacket, open where the zipper should
have been. I walked on and turned right at Nicollet, looked
back, and then walked through the swinging doors of
Woolworth's.

Without Neil in the Twin Cities, I missed Taos even more,
but I never spoke about it. How could I explain the modulation
of adobe in this land of brick duplexes and square lawns? If I

smelled wet pine in Minnesota, the smell would bring me back to Taos, to that big land, the sage, the cedar smoke, the sky, the sacred mountain. Friends wrote to me, "Come home. It's too cold to come up there to visit. Visit us down here." I'd fold their letters, put them back in their envelopes, and put them away in the top drawer of my bureau. I was still teaching in the public schools, but it had become dreary. I was tired of it. I thought, you can't go home again; this is where you are. I looked around at the thin-gray-carpeted duplex I lived in, the bare branches snapping against the window pane, and a shudder moved through me.

During this time I never went to Roshi. Suddenly, I who was so inquisitive had nothing to ask, nothing to say. I was stunned by the way life was unfolding. Though I often heard about impermanence in lecture, I couldn't bear experiencing it.

When I sat meditation, I cried about my grandmother. I worried who would sit shiva for her when she died. She was ninety-four years old now, in a nursing home on Long Island. All the relatives had left for Florida. Who would be there when she died? My body shook as I silenced sobs, tears running down my face in the white zendo. She had had a hip operation two years before and was spending the last of her days in bed and in a wheelchair among strangers. My grandmother? The one who told me stories:

"I stood in line with Mrs. Segal one Saturday to see the Rockettes. It was cold and we took turns standing in line and warming ourselves in the Horn and Hardart cafeteria across the street. Mrs. Segal wore a feathered hat. She'd say, 'Mrs. Edelstein, go inside. It's your turn to be warm.' We were polite, and though she was my best friend, in all the years I knew her, we always called each other by our last names."

One evening, I saw a photo on the front page of the

Minneapolis *Star Tribune* of a Jewish cemetery in Lodz, Poland. So many Polish Jews had been killed in concentration camps, the caption under the photo said, that there were more dead Jews in Lodz than live ones. I could see in the newsprint that the letters on the gravestones were carved in Hebrew. I looked at the picture a long time. My grandmother had come from Poland. The last time I'd seen her was two years ago, before the operation. When I mentioned visiting her, my mother would say, "She's completely senile now. It doesn't matter. She won't recognize you."

A garbage truck went by on the street. I looked up from the photo. I needed to see my grandmother again. I didn't care what shape she was in. I resolved to go.

As the bus made a full turn on the cloverleaf, headed from Newark Airport to the Port Authority terminal in Manhattan, I looked once, twice, out the window. I couldn't believe what I saw. There was a small flock—maybe seven—of pheasants, dark brown, heads bent, feeding on something in the yellow grass at the intersection of two busy highways. It was a good sign. The East Coast still had some magic.

From the Port Authority, I walked to Penn Station and took a train to Hicksville. At seven in the evening, I stepped off the train and took a cab to a cheap hotel that the cab driver suggested. I waited in my gold-and-turquoise room for the next morning when I would see my grandmother still alive. That night, I watched a sloppy movie on television about a cowboy shooting his lover's father and hiding out in the hills. I ordered a club sandwich from room service. I took a long bath in the pale yellow tub and saw mold forming on the ceiling.

I arrived at eight A.M. at the Polly Peterson Nursing Home. Polly was a rich woman who had left her mansion to the county twenty-eight years ago when she passed away. The county added on wings to the back of it, tore down the formal gardens and stuck up railings in the hallways.

"I'm sorry, no visitors until ten o'clock," they told me.

"Listen, my grandmother's here. I traveled from Minnesota just to see her. I haven't seen her in years. What room is she in?"

"She's in room 208. Take the back elevator, make a left, and go down the second hall."

"Thank you."

I ran past orderlies in white pushing carts of white bed sheets. The elevator door closed slowly and rose in its own sweet time to the second floor, where it opened with the speed of a flower. I jerked left and looked for the second hall. The corridor smelled of urine as though no amount of Lysol could remove it from the light pink cracking plaster walls. Old men and women sat in wheelchairs in the hall, screaming, while the nurses cleaned their rooms.

"Mother Jesus, Mother Jesus," yelled one woman with knotted white hair. "Help me. Help me."

I passed 207. The next room must be my grandmother's. I turned in. The room was light gray. A curtain sheet hung around her bed. I pulled the sheet aside. There she was. I stood over the bed and just looked, as though trying to adjust my eyes to darkness. She wasn't aware that I was there. She was blind. Cataracts had grown over her eyes. I had heard about it, but I had forgotten. There was a red rash on her forehead. No teeth. They'd taken away her false ones. Only three natural ones were still left on the bottom. No wedding ring, no earrings. My mother had taken all the jewelry, so no one would steal it. My grandmother was mumbling in Yiddish to herself.

I leaned my face close to hers, touched her on the shoulder. "Grandma, it's your granddaughter, Natalie." I was aware that no one had visited her in a long time. She turned her head and gazed in my direction. I began to cry. I touched her thin silver hair that was dirty and lying close to her skull.

"Grandma, do you know I love you?"

"Yes, I love you too. Tell me, who are you?"

"I am Natalie, your granddaughter."

"I don't know who she is. Tell me, who is she?"

"I love you, Grandma. I love you."

I rubbed my cheek next to hers. On impulse, I pulled down the bar of her bed, lifted up the sheets and climbed in next to her. Her breath was terrible. I asked her the same questions over and over.

"Who is your daughter, Helen? Who is Nathan? How many children did you have? Who is your husband? Where are you now? Who are you?"

"Darling, I don't remember."

She turned to me from time to time. "Have I ever met you?" A pause. "Oh, yes, Helen. I love her so. She is my husband."

She wanted water. I jumped out of bed to find water. Down the hall near the elevator, I found a fountain. No glass. I ran to the orderly.

"My grandmother is thirsty. She wants water."

He ambled over to a closet and brought back a plastic cup. I filled it and rushed back to her side. When I got there, she was surprised. She had forgotten about water. She drank it, because I put it to her lips. Then I climbed back into her bed and put my arms around her.

"Grandma, tell me a story," I beseeched her.

She answered, "About a glory?"

I said, "How to begin it?"

"There's nothing in it," she said.

She had tape loops in her mind, and if I began something

she had said many times in her life, she could respond out of some rote memory, though she didn't know what she was talking about. I was satisfied anyway. I was working up to get her to sing. She used to love to sing. So with my arms around her, lying next to her, I began to sing lines from every old song I could think of that she used to like.

"I love you, a bushel and a peck. Oh, my darlin' Clementine. A pretty girl is like a melody."

The nurse walked in at this point, saw me and left. I didn't care. I got quite exuberant singing, sure the nursing home hadn't heard anything like this in years.

Suddenly she joined in: "I like the likes of you. I do! I do! I do!" and her shoulders moved against the pillow. My grandmother stopped time. We heard a man's voice above us on the loudspeaker, asking for a nurse from the third floor.

My grandmother turned to me, laughing. "He thinks I'm singing to him!" She was fully aware. She grabbed my arm and touched me. I felt cells fly from her to me and back again. I clapped wildly. She was a great singer. The world was absolutely perfect. I kept clapping above our heads and my mouth filled with my tears. My grandmother hadn't lived beyond her time, as my relatives said, shaking their heads. Her time was right now. Again, my grandmother drifted off, but it had happened.

The nurse came in again. I had to leave for a while so they could clean the room. "After all, visiting hours don't begin until ten." She had to change my grandmother, who wore a diaper. The nurse informed me that there were coffee machines in the basement.

I walked down the hall toward the elevator. Someone screamed, "Mercy, mercy, Lord. Give me mercy." A nurse who didn't see me yelled, "Shut up!" It didn't ruffle the old lady's feathers one bit. I heard her bellowing it out again as the elevator door closed.

I got lost in the labyrinth of the basement corridors. Nurses, orderlies, janitors walked by, chatting. They were relaxed. The basement was theirs. Finally, I found the machines. Egg salad sandwiches in diagonal halves peered through plastic doors. The thickness of the egg salad was displayed between white bread. I didn't want any, nor did I want coffee. I pulled the knob for green LifeSavers.

Two broken orange chairs and a dark green vinyl one were piled near the candy machine. At the other end of the room, two orderlies and a nurse on their break watched "Give Us This Day" on the TV. Their legs were up on a coffee table in front of them and they drank something from a brown paper bag. I bought an ice cream sandwich. With a spoon, I could feed my grandmother the vanilla between the two hard wafers. She loved ice cream.

When I returned to the second floor, my grandmother was in the sun room with eighteen other patients in wheelchairs. Seven of them sat around two long tables; four of them had their heads lying on the table. No one talked. Some drooled. My grandmother was in a dress now, the old kelly green striped one. The zipper in the back was broken and closed by a safety pin. She sat quietly, her chin resting on her chest.

A woman in a thin red nylon sweater over a wool dress glided over in her wheelchair and repeated, "Darling, will you help me? Darling, will you help me? Darling, will you help me?" I asked her what she needed help with. "Take me home. Take me home with you to Carolina." I said I couldn't. "Darling, will you help me?" She grabbed my skirt. A nurse walked in and the woman who wanted to go to Carolina shifted her attention. I fed my grandmother the ice cream. She liked it.

Her room was ready. I wheeled her back and faced her in her wheelchair so she could look out the window, if only she could see. I slipped a green LifeSaver into her mouth. "Sweetheart, thank you. This is the most delicious thing I have ever tasted." It helped her bad breath. I kissed her and touched her face.

Her lunch was delivered. The ground-up food was on a white plate. There was a scoop of lumpless mashed potatoes, pure white, covered with a pale yellow gravy already solidifying from the cornstarch, ground beef and ground beets refined to the consistency of applesauce. My grandmother ate it all with no opinion. This was the same woman who never let us eat at McDonald's, because they couldn't possibly sell their hamburgers so cheap if it wasn't really horse meat they served up between those white buns. Because she was blind, I touched the spoon to her lips, so she could feel there was food and open her mouth. She forgot from spoonful to spoonful that she was eating. Intermittently, she drank milk directly from a half-pint container that I held and tilted for her.

I didn't want to leave her. Again and again, I told her I loved her. She must know at least that before I leave.

Someone rolled in for a moment. It was the woman from Carolina. "Darlin', would you help me, darlin', would you help me?" Then she rolled out to try someone in the hall.

It is four o'clock. I have to leave. I may never see her again. This may be the last time. Again, I begin our old repartee, when we used to lie in bed together: "Shall I tell you a story? About a glory? How to begin it? There's nothing in it." I kneel by her wheelchair. My chin is on her arm. She talks to herself. The sun is going down.

As I waited for the slow elevator, I looked down the hall. A man I could barely see in the pale, early evening light was seated at the end near the window. He played a harmonica, really slow. I knew the song: "In the pines, in the pines, where the sun never shines." He wore a light blue short-sleeved shirt. The elevator door opened as slowly as time and I entered.

I flew back to Minneapolis and still I did not go to Roshi. I saw him often in lecture; he sat zazen with us, but I had no personal contact with him to ask individual questions as I used to. I wasn't mad at him or disconnected from him. How often he had said in lecture, "Finally, there is nothing to say. Just sit down on your cushion and face the wall." I was listening to him now. I had nothing to say. I sat with my sorrow. The teachings were grinding into me.

PART
FOUR

After six years of living six blocks from the Minnesota Zen Meditation Center, I left. The original reason I had moved to Minneapolis—to be married—no longer existed. I wanted to leave the deep north, I was finished there. And Zen Center? I barely said good-bye. It seemed as though I left the zendo, almost the way water mixes with Kool-Aid. The water becomes red from the cherry flavor. I left colored for life. But red water doesn't know it's red. It has not met itself yet. I left not knowing what I had learned, but I knew I would never leave Zen. Though my personal life took a different direction, I carried Zen with me. I knew the dharma was bigger than the Minnesota Zen Center. Roshi had taught me that.

We have an illusion that a certain time, a certain place, a certain person is the only way. Without it or them, we are lost. It is not true. Impermanence teaches us this. There is no one thing to hold on to. Once, a few years earlier, I told Roshi in anger, "I'm never coming back here." He laughed and said, "The gate swings both ways. I cannot hold anyone." Yet, when I returned two months later, I could tell he was happy to see me, but he had to go beyond his personal likes and dislikes. He could not say to me, "Please, Natalie, don't go. I like you." He was my teacher. As a teacher, he had the responsibility to teach me, to put forth the depth of human existence, whether he or I liked it or not. "Meetings end in departures" is a quote from the early sutras of Shakyamuni. No matter how long the meeting or what the relationship, we depart from each other. Even marriage or monkhood, those lifelong commitments, end in

death. In the face of that truth, he said, "You can go or come."
He was not tossed away by personal preferences; it was his
practice to stand on something larger, regardless of his subjective
feelings. And if I returned, the choice had to be mine. I was
responsible for myself.

So I left Minnesota. I returned to New Mexico, but Roshi
came with me. I carried his teachings south down Interstate 35,
then out 90, past the exit to Blue Earth and Worthington, into
the tip of South Dakota, stopping at Costa's Café and eating at
the salad bar full of marshmallows, canned fruit salads, and small
cellophane packages of saltines. I carried his words, his friend-
ship, down highway 81 into Nebraska, lingering in Norfolk
among fertile fields and cows, with friends, Bob and Barbara,
who lived in a big white house, then along Interstate 80, going
west, past Kearney and North Platte, and then south through
Colorado, opening into my beloved big sage space of northern
New Mexico.

I never said good-bye formally to Roshi and I am sorry
for that. Though I carried him with me, our formal time of
teacher and student in Minnesota was over and I wish I had
expressed my gratitude. But I was ignorant. I didn't know it
was over. It seems to me now that I still didn't know anything.
Gratitude is a mature emotion. Only in the last year or two in
Minneapolis, with the divorce, did I start to digest the teachings
on a quieter, deeper level inside me. And at that time of my
departure, I was in too much pain to understand my relationship
with Roshi and what he had given me. I knew Roshi meant a
lot to me, but I thought he would always be around, the way
you think as a young child that your mother will be there, or
a house, a street you live on. We are naive, innocent when we
are children. I was still ignorant as an adult and as a Zen student.

Six years I had been there and still ignorant! We take a long time to learn some things.

Roshi once told us that there were three different kinds of horses: with one, just a tug at the reins made them start moving; the second, a kick in the flanks and they were off; and then there were those that had to be beaten to the bone with a whip before they started to move. "Unfortunately," he said, "most human beings are the third kind." He told us we act as though we were going to live forever. "Wake up," he said.

I drove my thick carcass out of Minnesota. I regret I did not thank him for his great effort, did not bow in front of him, present him with a little spice cake, an orchid, a wool cap to keep his shaved priest's head warm. I know he understood. He did not teach in order to receive anything, but gratitude may be the final blessing for a student. Thank you, thank you, thank you. I know what I have received. Knowing that, the duality of teacher and student dissolves. The teacher can pour forth the teachings; the student absorbs them. No resistance, no fight. It is a moment of grace.

Instead, most of us want more and more. We want to be recognized. We want our egos fed. To feel gratitude is to recognize the other, to lay down our own greed and aggression. What a relief! What joy!

But a teacher does not teach to receive presents. That is the work of a teacher, not to get caught in the likes or dislikes of a student, but to come forth always with the deepest teachings. Often the student does not like this, thinks the teacher is mean, unfeeling, but a good teacher knows that if he or she plants a real seed, someday, maybe years later, even in the most ignorant of students the seed may sprout. So the teacher's job is to close the gap between the student's ignorance and the teachings, but

often the student does not understand any of this. That is why
the student is a student. The teacher understands this. That is
why the teacher can have abundant patience.

But if the student doesn't know about the gap, how can
she learn? There is something in us, an urgency to meet the
teachings on the other side, that gnaws at our ignorance, that
desires to meet our own true face, however lazy and comfort-
loving we may seem to be. This something was working in me,
albeit slowly, and often underground.

When I arrived in Taos, I stayed for a month in a silver school
bus out on the mesa with my friends Gini and Michael. It was
wonderful to be back up in Taos, but I walked around there
like a ghost. I'd see a new restaurant and remember when it
was The House of Taos, a place where Neil and I hung out that
served the best green chili pizza, and where Ron, the owner,
stood in the back, tall and bearded, over the ovens. I'd see Taos
Valley School, now a private elementary school, and remember
when it was DaNahazli, the old hippie school where I taught
writing to barefoot kids wearing cantaloupe-seed necklaces, and
where Ram Dass would stop in when he was visiting Lama
Foundation, and where we did Sufi dancing every Friday afternoon in the playground. Taos wasn't the same, it was becoming
gentrified—no, that wasn't it. It was that almost everyone I
knew had left. I carried an old dream of it in my body, but
most of my friends had moved on to meditation centers in
Boulder, San Francisco, Los Angeles.

And Taos was also the same: There was the land, the
golden light, the ecstatic experience of being brought into the
moment with that huge sky behind you, the sacred mountain
of Taos ever present on the landscape. There was absolutely no

place else to be but where you were, watching that hummingbird feed on the pink hollyhock in front of you. Yes, this was still the best place. But I had left. I had met Katagiri Roshi, and now I was back, alone, carrying his practice with me.

I moved on after a month to stay with my friend Rob in Albuquerque, and while I was there I worked on *Writing Down the Bones*, which I had started a few months earlier in Minnesota. Each morning before I began to write, I walked along the irrigation ditch in the south valley of Albuquerque. The Sandias were in the distance to my left, in a blue-purple haze, and close up all around me were snarling, black dogs behind fences that also held old pickups, rundown adobe houses, chickens pecking at nails and pigweed, horses, goats, tires, and old bottles. I loved those walks, the pale soft yellow earth, the surprising rush of water, the delicate green of willows. I thought of that mile stretch along the ditch as one of my angel places. I felt good there, glad to be in New Mexico again near Twitty's Rib Hut and Consuelo's Chiles Rellenos.

After that month in Albuquerque, I settled in Santa Fe. It was the place I had the least attachment or connection with and so it seemed the least haunted by the past. I rented an adobe on Don Cubero Street.

"Make writing your practice," Roshi had told me.

"Oh, no, I can't. My brain," I pointed to my head, "I can't shut it up."

"If you commit to it, writing will take you as deep as Zen," he told me.

I settled into writing in Santa Fe. Sitting meditation seemed to fade away. Everything about my years in Minnesota fell away, except my relationship with Roshi. I hardly remembered the cold, the gray sky, the thunderous Mississippi, not because Minnesota hadn't been a deep time for me, but because I was so happy to be back in New Mexico, where I belonged. I do remember one day after being back several months, I suddenly ached for a white clapboard house on the corner of Emerson and Thirty-second. I'd never been in that house; I'd hardly noticed it, but it was on my route to the food coop and the zendo and it was catty-corner to the mailbox. I must have taken it in on a body level, and later after I left Minneapolis I spent a whole afternoon oddly aching for it, a symbol to me of the Midwest, plain clean lines, a second story, on a block with a square lawn, a wooden porch—different from the sage and rambling adobe of the Southwest.

I had never spoken about New Mexico in Minnesota, and now I didn't know how to explain my experience in the zendo—all that formal sitting—to my old friends in New Mexico. What could I say? I sat a lot. Yeah, so what did you learn? my friend would ask. We would be walking in an arroyo behind St. John's. The sky was turquoise; the earth, shades of pink; and there was red rock dotted with piñons. I don't know, I'd say. And I'd shake my head. It was all in me. It was nothing I could tell about. I did not learn computer programming or aerodynamics in the zendo. I wasn't sure yet how to apply it to my world. I was still working to digest it.

The only place in Santa Fe I felt comfortable writing in was The Haven, on Canyon Road. That was odd for me. Usually I could write any place, and The Haven was a bit high-priced, not a café, really, where you could just order tea, but more a full-meal restaurant with linen napkins. Yet, when I opened my notebook there, I was content to write *Bones*, to tell about writing practice, to share what Roshi had taught me. I was afraid to write the book, afraid that after divulging the deepest ways I saw writing and the world, everyone would laugh at me, so if I felt good at The Haven, I didn't question it. I went there often, ordered their cheapest lunch, and sat at the table near the window. I'd think to myself as I wrote, no one in Santa Fe knows Roshi. I'm alone here in this writing.

After I'd been going to The Haven for several weeks, the owner came up to me.

"Hi. I see you write here often. What are you writing?"

"Oh, a book about using writing as a practice, like Zen practice," I said.

"Oh, yeah, I'm a Zen student. I study with Baker Roshi at the Cerro Gordo zendo," she said.

"You do?" I asked, incredulous. "You must know Katagiri then. He's my teacher."

"Of course I do." She sat down at my table. She'd sat sesshin with Katagiri many times when he was in San Francisco. She then proceeded to tell me about her recent trip to Japan and how she had visited Dogen's ashes at his monastery, Eiheiji. She turned her head. "You know, most of the cooks and waiters here are Zen students."

"You're kidding."

She nodded her head. "Hey, Robert, come over." She pointed to me. "She studied with Katagiri." Then she turned back to me. "Oh, come and write any time. You're welcome here."

I was delighted. No wonder I felt good about writing my book here. My instincts were strong. I had found a safe place.

In the spring, I began working at The Haven as a part-time cook. I needed the money and I was having a hard time with the writing of *Bones*. I had suddenly become very afraid of failure—and just as afraid of success. I watched myself avoid the notebook as if it were a plague. Getting a job will be a good thing, I thought to myself. I became the dessert cook. I marveled over my chocolate mousses, chocolate cakes. I licked my fingers often. Chocolate became the basic ingredient in all the desserts except the flan. For two months, I enjoyed the job, my coworkers, the new activity. Then I became tired of it. What am I doing with my life? I'd ask. What about the book?

I'd just broken up with a boyfriend I dated for six months. After only two weeks, he'd already found someone else. It made me mad.

"But you didn't want to be with him," my friends kept saying.

"I know," I said, "but it doesn't matter. How could he find someone so quickly?"

One night at my most depressed the phone rang as I iced a cake. I picked it up. "The Haven—can I help you?"

It was my friend Janet in Albuquerque. I was surprised. "Listen, Nat, a bunch of us are going down to the jazz festival in New Orleans. We have an extra ticket. Why don't you come? It will cheer you up. You've been so down."

"I can't afford it," I said. "I have a book to write." Meanwhile, I wasn't writing. It felt like a term paper due in school that I had hanging over my head. It wasn't that the writing was hard. I was afraid to complete it, to finish it.

Janet insisted. "Oh, come on, Nat. We'll have a great time."

"Okay, I'll do it," I said and hung up, looking for people in the kitchen who would substitute for me for that week.

I drove down to Albuquerque that Thursday. We were all going to meet at Rob's—there were six of us. I was an hour early. I decided I'd take a walk along the ditch where I'd been a year earlier. I walked for ten minutes, felt the soft earth beneath my shoes. Suddenly I began to shake and fell down crying, my face right down there in the dirt. "You've got to finish that book. You've got to finish that book," an inner voice cried. I pounded my fist on the ground. "You've got to do it for Roshi, for all he gave you. I don't care if you're afraid. Finish it." I wept and wept as those fierce black dogs behind their fences growled and barked.

When I got up, I brushed myself off. There was resolve in my body as I walked back to Rob's.

We flew to Louisiana, and during the whole music festival I sat in the gospel tent, right up close to the stage. I couldn't believe the sound coming out of those Christian women, how a chest could be that big and open, and how huge a voice it could produce.

When I returned home, I quit cooking at The Haven; I quit everything else I was doing. I wrote seven days a week for seven weeks, rarely leaving that little adobe on Don Cubero. I moved through the book. No resistance, no thought; I just kept writing. I pulled the last page from my typewriter on a Sunday evening and knew it was finished.

During the time I was struggling with *Bones*, I taught writing workshops in my living room. I knew most people in Santa Fe hadn't known anyone like Roshi and I was surprised, though the town was a New Age mecca, how few people had sat meditation. I realized zazen was an old-fashioned kind of thing and hard. Simple things my students in my writing classes did not know. I told them to ground themselves in detail. They argued with me. They wanted to write about the cosmic world. I said, "Give me the details of drinking a cup of mint tea. That's cosmic enough." I told them to continue whether it was hard or easy. Often they said no and drifted to other things. I made up a motto for them—"With your feet in the clouds and your head on the ground."

I took a so-called New Age workshop in my first year back. Its advertisement said, "You want to go fast. You're unlimited." Well, it sounded good, but then I stopped to think: We're all exhausted from going fast. Who's unlimited? I'm not. I'll die someday. I'm in a human body. When I stopped to argue this with a group member, she said, "Well, the psyche grows fast." No, it doesn't, I thought. Look at history. We are dumb and slow; the sins of the fathers and mothers are carried on by the children, and only through our willingness to slow down and examine can we feel the effects of alcoholism, incest, rage, hatred, greed, and lumberingly change our behavior.

That statement that the psyche grows fast was unrooted, wasn't connected with the the earth. A tree has a growth spurt, but it is grounded by the depth of its roots. That New Age workshop borrowed from Zen, from religion; I heard watered-down statements that were directly out of Buddhism, but they were empty of the spiritual connection. Something smart from religion was taken for the sake of self-aggrandizement and pleasure. I worried about my Santa Fe writing students, thinking that one moment they'd take a writing workshop and the next moment they'd go on to Rolfing as a way to save themselves. No practice was taught at that workshop. By the end of the weekend, everyone was salivating, drooling with their own ecstasy, but by Monday or Tuesday morning they were flat out, deflated, depressed. They had no way of integrating what they had learned and no way of maintaining it—except, of course, by signing up for another high-cost weekend.

I told my writing students that practice is something done under all circumstances, whether you're happy or sad. You don't become tossed away by a high weekend or a blue Monday. It is something close to you, not dependent on high-tech gyrations or smooth workshop-leader talk. Writing is something you do quietly, regularly, and in doing it, you face your life; everything comes up to fight, resist, deny, cajole you. Practice is old-fashioned, not hip or glamorous, but it gets you through Monday, and it lets you see the ungroundedness of hyped-up New Age workshops or quick ways to write a best-selling novel that you end up never writing.

After I had been in Santa Fe a year, I went back to visit Minneapolis and I made an appointment to see Roshi. I brought him an Acoma Pueblo pot. I wanted him to have something of New Mexico. It was hand-done, smooth, brown and white, with a black line design on it. I loved Acoma. The old pueblo was built on top of a mesa and was called Sky City.

I walked into Roshi's study. There he was, softer, kinder than I remembered him. It was summer. He wore a white tee-shirt, and I noticed the skin at the base of his neck had gathered a little. He was growing older.

"Roshi, they're crazy in Santa Fe. I need a teacher again." I was afraid I'd soon be gobbled up by Santa Fe, seduced into a hundred different things: aura balancing, shamanic journeys, crystal readings, rebirthings, past-life regressions. I needed a teacher to keep me on the path.

"Don't be so greedy," he said when I told him I wanted a teacher. "Writing is taking you deep." He tapped the *Bones* manuscript I brought to show him. "Keep writing. You can write or visit me, if you need to."

No teacher? That was too lonely. Out there alone with my writing? Then he told me, "Anything you do deeply is lonely. Even the Zen students here," he said, "the ones who are going deep are very lonely."

I nodded. I understood, though I didn't want to. It was

up to me now, and it was true that the writing of *Bones* had
taken me deep. In the act of writing, alone at my old oak dining
room table on Don Cubero Street, I had begun to close the gap
between what Roshi was saying all those years and my own
understanding of it. Writing was the vehicle for making the
teachings mine, for knitting them close to me.

When *Bones* was published a year later, a Zen monk, Steve
Hagen, who knew me all those years in Minnesota and who
read it, asked me in amazement, "Did you know all this stuff
when you were practicing here?"

I smiled. I knew I had been quite a misbehaved student.
"No," I said. "Writing taught it to me."

When I returned to Santa Fe after visiting Roshi, an ac-
quaintance asked, "What did you do up there?"

"I gave a reading," I said.

"Astrological?" she inquired.

"No, poetry," I answered.

Once I went to Roshi when I lived in Minnesota and told him,
"When I'm at Zen Center, I feel like a writer. When I'm with
writers, I feel like a Zen student."

"Someday you will have to choose. You're not ready yet,
but someday you will be. Writing and Zen are parallel paths,
but not the same."

We never spoke about it again. I continued to write; I
continued to sit.

Three months after I finished *Bones*, I went camping alone
one weekend in August by the Chama River. I wondered why
I insisted on going alone, since I'd just met a man I really liked
in Santa Fe. The whole weekend I anticipated some vision or

epiphany I was supposed to have. I woke Sunday morning to the loud gallop of deer hooves inches from my head. I'd slept out in a sleeping bag on the ground, no tent, and the deer were heading for the river. There must have been fourteen of them. I'd never seen them from that angle before: black hooves, beige bodies. Mostly I was panicked. By the time I sat up, I saw the last of them crashing through the willows at the Chama's edge.

I thought, this must be it, the epiphany: I was almost trampled to death. I can leave now. I made a breakfast of brown rice and roasted nuts over a fire and then packed up. I had to drive eleven miles on winding, rutted dirt roads before I hit the blacktop. Pink cliffs shot up from the dry desert to my left and the Chama River and its valley spread out to my right.

I'd gone about three miles when suddenly I burst out crying. At the same instant, my blue Rabbit, which had never done this before, overheated, and steam shot up with great force from the hood of the car. I cried; it steamed. I repeated over and over: "I chose being a writer. I chose being a writer," and sobbed and sobbed. Before that moment I had no idea that that question had been working in me so deeply. Though I had written a book and talked about writing practice, I still never consciously considered myself a writer rather than a Zen student.

That talk with Roshi had occurred maybe six years earlier. I had forgotten it, but beings seen and unseen and our wild minds continue to work while we are busy apparently only shaking salt on our french fries. I felt a great relief after that morning by the Chama. I drove back to Santa Fe, stopping in Tesuque for a wonderful meal all by myself at El Nido's.

Why did I have to choose? I don't know if we do really choose. Eventually, I think, something chooses us and we shut up, surrender, and go with it. And the difference between Zen and writing? In writing you bring everything you know into writing. In Zen you bring everything you know into nothing, into the present moment where you can't hold on to anything.

It's a great challenge to write about a place you lived in while you are still living in it, to have perspective on it. It's not impossible. It's been done and done beautifully. After all, it is only in the last century that we've had such freedom of travel and movement. And I imagine if we don't change place, time is always changing anyway, so we are always looking back over our shoulder at the past, something that is no longer here, as we write.

But not being in the close physical vicinity of Roshi, not meeting my own resistances head on, having the distance and time, my appreciation for Roshi deepened, flowered. I was no longer doing *my* work, *my* books, *my* writing workshops; I was doing his work, our books; I was teaching writing to help all sentient beings. I was teaching it the way he taught me Zen. He inspired me, gave me a vision of a way to be.

Sometimes at the beginning of a writing workshop, I'd look out at my students and think, Oh, no, I don't want to start again, all over, another group. I've been doing this for years. Then I'd think, did Roshi not put up with you, no, not "put up with," treat you like a Buddha consistently under all circumstances? Yes, I'd nod. Well, get out there, I'd say, and I'd begin my class with gratitude.

Once over tea with a friend in Santa Fe—it was November, the month was important, the branches were bare, a few birds darted past the window, I wore sweaters one over another, and the wood stove was crackling—I held the teacup in both my hands, and I remembered something. I began to tell my friend who was sitting there with me:

"You know, in Minnesota sometimes it can be this cold in early October." I paused. "Once I was on the Zen center's land in southeastern Minnesota, near New Albin, Iowa. We planned to build a permanent monastery there eventually, but at the time we sat a weekend sesshin in a big army tent. It was after lunch, we had work period and we all lined up and the work leader announced who would be doing what job. He said, 'Natalie and—I don't remember who the other person was—go over and carry the wood from up the hill down to the creek.' We were in silence. You didn't say, 'Oh, I don't want to do that,' you just did it. It was part of the training. So we went up and there were these huge tree trunks that had been cut down." I stood up in the kitchen and showed her how long the trunks were. "From here"—I paced the distance from the side cupboard door to the living room— "to here. And they were this big around." I showed her with my arms two and a half feet.

"My work partner motioned me in silence to get to the back end of a trunk and together we'd lift it up on our shoulders and carry it down. Well, I knew that it was impossible for me to do it. I can't remember who I was with, but he was huge— probably was a football player in college. I couldn't think 'impossible'—I couldn't think. I'd freak out. So I just did it. I walked across this long field with that huge trunk. If I thought, I would panic and the trunk would come crashing on top of me. At one point we passed Neil. He was raking. I saw him out of the corner of my eye. I think he stopped dead and was staring with his mouth open." My friend and I laughed. "But I didn't dare look at him. No thought. No thought. I just had to keep walking with that trunk."

Later my friend and I took a walk. When we got to the top of a hill, she turned to me. "You know, I realize you did something in Minnesota. You were gone and now you're back, so I forget those years, but something happened."

I nodded. It was true. And I remembered more about that weekend. I had seen wild turkeys up the hill in the afternoon, and the full moon crested the bluff near the Mississippi just as we stepped out from evening zazen.

The next morning had been very cold. There was frost on the bell. We hadn't expected it to get that cold that early in the year. After all, we slept and sat in tents. After the two periods of zazen beginning at five A.M., I was signed up to be the breakfast server. Servers never wore socks or gloves. I had to bow, barefoot, with my big pot of steaming rice in front of each student, then kneel on the ground and serve them—they were all sitting on the floor on cushions—then lug up the pot and go to the next person. I was cold. Roshi was the last person to be served. I couldn't wait to get it over with, to run out of the tent and put on my socks and gloves. As I knelt in front of Roshi, about to scoop a ladle of rice into his bowl, he sharply, clearly said to me, "Eat the cold." I took a deep breath, slowed down, and tried to open to weather. This man wasn't kidding around. Don't run away, not even from cold—digest it, he was saying. And he meant this for all my life, not just the moment I was there.

Now I was a thousand miles away from him. My deep love for him bound me to the teachings, kept me in them when I forgot them, now that I was back in New Mexico, far from the Minnesota zendo.

That is one of the things a teacher does for a student. She gives the student a personal connection to the teachings. They are no longer abstract high ideals. They are real. The Buddha dharma became a reality for me, because I saw Katagiri Roshi living it.

This is no different from an English teacher sharing a poet

with you. Mr. Clemente read Dylan Thomas and Brother Antonius aloud to us at the beginning of class and said, "I like this." I liked Mr. Clemente and I wanted to hear what he liked. It is much harder—almost impossible—to enter the teachings, even of poetry, on our own. Somewhere along the way someone showed us the beauty of one poem, so then we could enter other poems.

Jack Kerouac, the famous Beat author who wrote *On the Road*, read the Buddhist sutras and tried to sit meditation alone without a teacher. It was too hard. He did not succeed in any regular practice. He died an alcoholic, choking on his own vomit in Florida, living with his mother.

But, of course, being on the Buddhist path is no guarantee. We each have to eat the teachings ourselves. I remember Roshi telling me that there were ten monks ordained when he was ordained. One was now in jail; one went crazy and now was in a mental hospital; one physically attacked his teacher; and one committed suicide. He didn't know what had happened to the others. "Life is no guarantee," he said often. "You must make effort."

I finished *Writing Down the Bones* and began a novel, *Banana Rose*. I left Santa Fe, moved back to Taos, and had a solar one-room house built on the mesa next to my friends Gini and Michael. I went up to Minnesota about once a year, and when I was there, I'd visit Roshi. There he is, I'd think to myself when I saw him. Still here. Still studying the sutras, still sitting.

I asked him a question. "You know, Roshi, I'm writing a novel. Some of it's about me and Neil. I think I'm still protecting him. My friends say, 'You have to tell the truth.' I don't want to hurt him. I'm not writing the book to be mean."

Roshi didn't hesitate. He nodded. "Yes, you have to tell the truth."

Then his face lit up. "Don't worry. You won't hurt Neil, you'll help him. He'll read the book and know you better. He'll read the book and know what a woman is."

I smiled. My face lit up. He gave me tremendous permission. "Thank you," I said and that one short interview carried me easily for a year. I brought it home to Taos, chewed at it, shared it with my students: "If you write the truth, it doesn't hurt people, it helps them. They know you better."

Roshi went on sabbatical for a year to Japan. I was deep in *Banana Rose*, drinking mint tea at the Garden Restaurant every morning, while I kept my hand moving across the page, parking my car at an angle through the snow slush on the Taos plaza, walking out into the open sunlight at one o'clock after I was done writing. It sounds simple now. It was hard. Writing that novel, staying with it, was one of the hardest things I'd ever done. Knowing that it was a practice, that a practice was something you continued under all circumstances—Roshi had trained me in this—was what kept me going. I was making the teachings mine.

I finished the second draft of *Banana Rose* in January 1989. For several months, Roshi had been back in Minnesota from his sabbatical, and I heard he wasn't feeling well. He was in and out of the hospital. Pneumonia? Tuberculosis? There were many rumors. When I called Zen Center, everything was vague. This vagueness protected me.

Right before I flew to Baja in Mexico to hop a boat to follow the blue whales as a celebration for finishing my novel, I heard the word "cancer" on the long distance telephone wire that stretched from Minnesota to New Mexico. Cancer. My mind stopped. Cancer. It stunned me. The word echoed in my hollow skull. Cancer. Cancer. No mention of anything fatal. Chemotherapy. Radiation. "Roshi's in good spirits," the long-distance voice said. "He'll be all right." Cancer. I hung up the phone. Cancer. My whole bone structure dissolved and anything else that held me up on two feet. I don't remember if I cried then or not. At that moment it was deeper than crying.

Several times we caught sight of the blue whales. Their tails, their enormous backs. I was the only one aboard who did not bring a camera, who viewed those animals with her naked eye. The rest of the passengers snapped picture after picture, never taking their face from the lens. I planned to buy a few postcards when we hit land. I was sure a professional photographer had snapped a good one.

At night, when everyone was asleep below, I climbed on the upper deck, squatted by the rail, looked out at the sea, the amazing star-studded night sky, and I cried. I repeated over and over, "Please don't die. Please don't die."

At the same time I felt that this was the destiny of my teacher, the man who worked so hard to bring the dharma to America. He was only sixty-one years old. I had lived as though I had years left with this man. I'd never said it to myself before, but crying those nights on the deck I knew I loved this person more than anyone I had ever loved, and the love was full, clean, not broken by resentment, no holding back—this teacher had been able to pull that kind of love out of me. My heart poured forth with gratitude. If he was dying, I didn't know what I would do without him. Though I hadn't lived in Minnesota for four and a half years, Roshi was still my guiding light. I had no other model but him, though I think I never thought it possible to be like him.

In interviews and classes and among friends, people have asked me over the years, "So whom do you admire? Who are your models?" My response was singular, "Katagiri Roshi." Katagiri Roshi? What about women—Rosa Luxemburg? Gloria Steinem? No, Katagiri Roshi. What about writers? Eudora Welty? Willa Cather? Colette? Yes, I like them; they're fine, too, but for me everything paled next to Roshi, a small Japanese man who spoke broken English. I could go into dokusan, speak to him straight, and be answered straight. And never for a moment did I have to be concerned about him crossing a sexual boundary. I did not have to close down or protect myself. This is no small feat given the sexual transgressions of many spiritual teachers today. I needed that freedom to find myself, a place to step out whole, to be treated whole. I was in the presence of someone who was paying attention. Paying large attention. As though you suddenly planted the sun into a seat in a busy café and it beamed there. Think of that power, to work like the sun. The café would get quiet; everyone would turn toward it. And this power is in all of us: to shine in our heavens.

But I wasn't idealistic. My feelings were grounded in reality: I knew Roshi had trouble expressing his emotions; he clashed with some of the students; some thought he was too rigid, old-fashioned; the sangha was sometimes narrow, slow, did not reflect his magnanimity. Finally, he was disappointed in the midwestern students' commitment and in their inability to raise the money to realize his dream of a permanent monastery near New Albin, Iowa:

> I wish to build a place and an environment to promote the quiet sangha life in unity. We have some land, and I want to construct a building there to practice the Way revering the old ways. I think that

the mode of old ways reveals the modern one from a different aspect. Modern life is artificially protected. When the artificial environment collapses, for instance in a natural disaster or an economic calamity, people suffer severely. Modern people, therefore, need to live in direct contact with nature and find a practice method in tune with nature's rhythm. Old ways of life fit this purpose. Such a life will put the modern life in a different perspective and teach us how we should live. Therefore, I am convinced we must build such a practice place in America.

But he was patient, he continued.

And now he had cancer. Finally, in May, it dawned on me that I should visit. I think I wanted everything to get better long distance, for him to be healed, and then I could forget his mortality. I was in denial, scared. He was getting out of the hospital after a long series of chemotherapy treatments and complications. I called ahead of time to let him know I was coming. He asked Tomoe, his wife, to request that I give a poetry reading at Zen Center while I was there, to lift people's spirits. I said, "Of course," but all I really wanted to do was see him. I would be happy just to have tea with him for ten minutes. I knew he wasn't well. I braced myself for seeing him. I knew he might look very different; old, thin, tired.

I brought his favorite shortbread cookies and small purple flowers—he loved any kind. We sat in his living room. We joked. He looked beautiful. It was hard to believe that he was so ill. I told him I loved him. He nodded. I told him, "When you were well, I didn't miss you. It was okay that I was so far away, but now I miss you all the time." He nodded.

That night, I read in the zendo. He didn't come down; I

didn't expect him to, but a long time later Tomoe told me he lay down on a blanket on their living room floor, which was above the zendo, so he could hear me. He hoped I would sing a funny song I'd written many years earlier that he liked, about being on the Zen center's land. It was called "Boodie Land." I was surprised. I didn't even remember the song anymore. I never knew it meant so much to him. I remember thinking at the time I wrote it that it might be a bit disrespectful or sacrilegious.

Two days after that reading, I returned to New Mexico, but now even my darling state couldn't hold me. It was as though all my cells turned toward that one northern midwestern city that held my teacher. I sent presents each week: wooden birds from Mexico, a turquoise and gray Pendleton blanket, a Zuni amber coyote fetish with a turquoise arrow at its heart indicating healing. Still, when I called Zen Center, it was hard to figure out what was going on. He completed chemotherapy and radiation treatments. They were waiting to see if his cancer went into remission. Tomoe called me early one morning, ecstatic, "The tests show no more cancer."

I went into a cautious relief. I dreamed that night that I was walking round and round Zen Center, that I was keeping guard. That morning, I decided that after I finished *Wild Mind*, the new book I was working on, I'd go up there for a few months and help out. If he was healing, I'd help him heal, and if he was dying—please, no—I'd help him do that. There was no place else I wanted to be, but near him.

Two or three weeks after Tomoe's call, I received another one. "They found cancer again." More chemotherapy, but the Zen students were optimistic. Roshi was on a pure diet; he was doing visualizations, receiving special acupuncture treatments.

At the end of September—I had one more month until I could move up there—the word "dying" was mentioned on the long distance wire. I hung up. The word I knew to be behind every thought but was not said, now was said. I sat down on the couch and I cried as though the earth poured out of me. That afternoon I was supposed to take a small Mesa Airlines plane to Albuquerque from the Taos airport seven miles from my home. Then I was to take a cab to the Pyramid Hotel and give a talk the next morning to a conference of English teachers. I had two hours until the plane left. I was crying so hard I left logic—I couldn't calculate how long I needed to get to the plane and coordinate that with the hands on the clock over my refrigerator. I drove those seven miles as though my car were Jell-O and I was sliding across a vista of sage brush. I pulled into the Taos airport just as they were closing the door on the plane. I ran down the runway and they let me on. We flew over the Rio Grande gorge and over country I knew well, but I'd never seen it from this angle: There were Dixon, Velarde, the apple orchards. Roshi wasn't dead yet, not yet, not yet. There was time.

I checked in at the Pyramid and went straight to my room. I was on the sixth floor, overlooking a golf course. It was early evening. I sat and stared out the big window that did not open and watched night descend over my sky. I did not leave the room. I did not sleep. I cried through most of the night. I didn't prepare a talk. The next morning I wore sunglasses to the lectern—my eyes were swollen. I took a deep breath, removed the dark glasses and looked at three hundred teachers. I hoped something would come. To my surprise, I talked about pleasure, about teaching out of pleasure, of teaching what you love. The audience was pleased. I put the sunglasses back on and headed for the back of the room and out to a cab at the front of the hotel. I flew back to Taos and though I was driving up to Minnesota in a month for a long stay, I made plane reservations for the coming weekend. I wanted to go up there and I didn't want to wait.

Unbeknownst to me, a group of twelve, the monks whom Roshi had ordained and Yvonne Rand, who had also studied with him, were called into Minneapolis that weekend. Plans for dharma transmission, the carrying on of the lineage, were being made. Roshi wasn't strong enough to do the whole ten-day ceremony, so his close friend Tsugen Narasaki Roshi was going to come in from Japan in December to perform it. This weekend, before he might become too weak, Roshi was to perform the part of the ceremony—eye-to-eye with the teacher—that was essential to take place with him in order for the transmission to be legitimate.

Shoken and Nonin, two American monks, flew in from Japan. Someone flew in from Milwaukee; another person from St. Louis; Yvonne Rand, from California. Most of the monks I had known before their ordinations, when they were Floyd and Mike, Janet and Roberta, before they took on their dharma names, Shoken, Dosho, Joen, Teijo.

I don't even remember getting to see Roshi that weekend—he was too sick, conserving his strength for the ceremony, but I was so happy to be there, near him, among my old friends. I felt like the thirteenth monk. I joined them for dinner; they invited me into the Buddha hall to chant with them. They thought Roshi would do the ceremony from his bed, but Roshi insisted on dressing in full regalia, in his special silk monk robes, and they told me he sat in full lotus as he performed the ceremony for each monk individually.

Some of the monks had drifted from Zen Center over the years, had gotten involved with family life and children.

Suddenly everyone was called together, called out of their homes and jobs to receive this dharma transmission, probably too early, too young in their practice, but Roshi might be dying—still the word was hardly mentioned. Roshi said he did it this way so things would not become political, so the transmission would be spread out among several people. He said no one was ready; over time, someone might emerge as a teacher.

It was during that weekend that Nonin remembered he was the one carrying those big logs with me on the Zen land that weekend. He was Don Chowaney then. "I wondered why you were so scared." He laughed. "Of course, look how much smaller you are than me." It was that weekend that I began to regret not having been ordained as a monk, only so I, too, could have eye-to-eye with my dearest teacher.

On Monday, I flew back to New Mexico and worked hard to finish *Wild Mind*. Those few weeks were a blur for me. I was racing against time, against the heartbeat and breath of my teacher. I sent the manuscript to my editor, locked up my house, packed up my car and drove north through Colorado and Nebraska. I remember staying in a hotel in Nebraska, near Kearney, that had free videos. I watched *Gone with the Wind* late into the night, and the next morning sped on to Minnesota.

I settled into my friends', Joni and Cary's, house on York Avenue—they had an extra bedroom—and I made a vow to go to Zen Center each day, whether anyone else was there or not, and to make myself useful. I was assured I couldn't see Roshi: he was too sick. I didn't expect to see him; I wanted to help.

The first day on my way to Zen Center I stopped and picked up some purple violets at a florist's and brought them over.

"Go ahead up and put them in Roshi's apartment. He's at radiation treatment. He'll be back in an hour," one of the Zen students told me.

I filled a vase in the kitchen and placed the flowers on the coffee table. I looked around. Flowers that people had sent or dropped off were everywhere, on the kitchen table, near the sink, on a dish cabinet, on two window sills. I went downstairs to the basement to help collate newsletters.

An hour later someone came downstairs. "Natalie, Roshi's back. He lay down on the couch, pointed at those flowers you brought, and asked, 'Who brought those?' When we told him you were here, he told us to send you up."

I went up. There he was, on the couch. I knelt next to him. He still looked so beautiful, his face radiated. He took my hands.

I said, "I'm here to help *you* now. I'll be here a while."

He nodded. "Dress warm. It's cold in Minnesota. You can catch a cold. Be careful."

"Yes," I said. I nodded. "Rest now," and he closed his eyes. I left him and went downstairs.

On the bulletin board in the basement a small sign was pinned up:

Just
to be
is a
blessing.

Just

to

live

is

holy.

Abraham Joshua Heschel

I read it every day I was there.

On the third day, as I left the house, Joni said, "Nat, are you dressed warmly enough? It's very cold. The thermometer says twenty below, already, and it's not December."

"That's okay," I said cheerily. Joni looked at Cary in amazement. I, who was miserable in the cold when I lived there, didn't care. I was happy. I was near Roshi. If a great light was going out and these were his last days, I wanted to be near him. There was no place else on earth I wanted to be.

I went over to Zen Center. "Nat, we need help sewing the priest robes upstairs." I went upstairs. Special robes were needed for the transmission ceremony in a few weeks. I stood in the doorway of the sewing room. It was a square white room across from the kitchen, empty but for a blue carpet and a chest of drawers in the corner. Tomoe was kneeling on the floor across the room near the window, a large piece of dark brown material spread out in front of her. She was stitching. She looked up and across the vast room at me. Oh, no! Here we were, so many years later, the two of us, about to sew again.

Ten years earlier, I had stitched a *rakusu* by hand. It was my lay ordination robe. A rakusu is a biblike garment, worn around the neck that symbolizes the Buddha's robe. It is patterned after a rice field, which holds all of life—water, rice, human beings, insects, sky, sun. It was intricate to sew. I was not a good seamstress. A group of us met twice a week for several months to sew them. The sewing itself was a practice. With each stitch we were to repeat silently: "I take refuge in the Buddha." I seek protection and sanctuary in Buddhism. I said this in my mind as I lifted the needle's black thread in and out of the black material on my lap. But I was restless, impatient. Mostly I had no idea about the depth of lay ordination. I did it because it presented itself. Like everything else I figured I'd understand later. One evening, I had finally caught up to where everyone else was in their sewing.

I held up my black material. "Hey, look," I said to people at my table.

Marilyn looked at it. "Nat, the stitches are so big!" They were supposed to be small. I had galloped ahead with my needle to catch up.

"Oh, who cares," I said. "It's all right."

At that moment, Tomoe leaned across the table, grabbed the rakusu out of my hand, ripped open all the stitches, and handed it back to me. "Do it again," she said.

My mouth fell open, tears stung my eyes. I leaned over the material and tried to match the two black cottons together again. I was thick-skinned, stubborn: Over the next few weeks, I finished in time for ordination.

But here I was ten years later with Tomoe, about to sew. I now understood these were Buddha's robes we were handling. I would try harder, but I knew in the past ten years I hadn't become a better seamstress. Except for an occasional button that fell off a shirt, my rakusu was the last thing I'd sewn. I stepped into the room.

Tomoe showed me what to do. She, too, remembered my rakusu. She brought it up. "I'm sorry," she said. "I didn't mean to hurt you."

"Oh, it was my fault," I said.

"No, it was mine," she said. "It was all my ignorance."

It was as though she had turned the whole incident inside out. From the way she said it, I saw that she felt no better or different than me. I was touched.

Three years after I took lay ordination, I went to Roshi. "I'm ready to take bodhisattva vows." A bodhisattva is someone who vows to return lifetime after lifetime to help all sentient beings and who does not enter nirvana until everyone goes before her.

Roshi laughed. "You've already taken them."

"When?" I asked.

"When you took lay ordination." He laughed and laughed.

Since I had driven to Minnesota, I had a car. Tomoe didn't drive, so in those first weeks I ended up driving her around a lot on the frozen Minneapolis streets and out to suburban malls I'd never been to before.

On one drive, she turned to me. "I remember the first time I met you."

"You do?" I asked, amazed.

"Yes, it was at the Blue Heron restaurant." The Blue Heron was a Zen Center restaurant that I worked at when I first moved to Minnesota. "I looked up over the counter at you"—Tomoe was short, maybe five feet—"and kept repeating my order and you kept saying 'What?' You couldn't understand my English. I thought, She'll never understand. You were wearing a red shirt and I thought I'd never seen such bright eyes."

Just then I turned a corner at Hennepin and Thirty-sixth. I gulped. You noticed me, I thought. Someone paid that much attention? "You remembered my shirt color. Wow, you must have a good memory."

"When you don't speak English well and you've just come to this country, everything is so difficult, you remember every-thing." She also remembered a time she corrected me for eating the *gomasio*—the salty sesame seasoning used in the formal oryoki meals—right out of the dish. I realized people were paying attention, that all the students at Zen Center mattered.

I drove Tomoe to buy gifts. The Japanese give gifts for everything. We had to buy gifts for Narasaki Roshi, who was coming from Japan, and his several assistants.

All of Zen Center was buzzing with preparations for dharma transmission. It was a very formal ten-day ceremony— private, only for the monks and the visiting Japanese teachers— and we had to raise money for all of it. Still, there were days when I was the only one downstairs. And Tomoe and Roshi were upstairs in their apartment, he sick in bed, she busy, busy with preparations.

One afternoon, Tomoe ran downstairs—I was in the zendo—"Please open this." It was a bottle. She needed it for Roshi's lunch. Another late afternoon—I remember how dark it already was outside; the sun so rarely shone in Minnesota; it was late November—Tomoe came down to the office. "Would you write a thank-you note to Milton Clapp? Ten years ago Roshi married him—he lives in North Carolina—and he gave us a beautiful piece of wood. We used part of it then for the altar in the zendo. Now the rest of it is being used as part of a special chair for the transmission ceremony. He should know what happened to the wood and we should thank him again."

Uh-huh, I nodded my head. She went back upstairs. What? I thought. Someone gave Roshi a piece of wood ten years ago and Tomoe's kept track of it and we're telling the gift giver what's happened to part of it ten years later? At the same time, she's taking care of her husband, who has cancer? I wrote the thank-you note, put a stamp on it, and mailed it.

Roshi insisted that the ceremony be done with full formality. He wanted to make sure that his dharma heirs were accepted at Soto Zen headquarters in Japan, where they were quite conservative and bureaucratic. We went along with his wishes.

For one part of the ceremony, we had to drape the entire zendo in red material. Then, in that new chair built with wood from Milton Clapp, Roshi was transformed into Vairochana, a source Buddha who was able to turn the root addiction of hatred into perfect wisdom. For one evening Roshi was transformed from a seemingly informal, accessible, and down-to-earth person, who at that time had cancer in his human body, into a very formal, symbolic, and powerful person. This was supposed to take place at midnight. It happened at night but earlier, because of Roshi's illness. I'm not sure about all this, because those who were not monks were not allowed to attend.

I shared the cooking responsibilities for those ten days with another Zen student. We made three meals a day for about twenty people. We were there from five in the morning until seven at night. Near the end of those ten days, I also taught a weekend writing workshop to help raise money for the ceremony.

The evening the teachers from Japan arrived—it was a Thursday—we had a formal early tea for them before they went to bed to sleep off their tremendous jet lag.

Right after the quiet, slow tea, the man I was dating picked me up and we went off to a Rolling Stones concert with fifty thousand people in the Metrodome. That was how I coped with the energy at Zen Center. I juxtaposed the pressure we were under there—my teacher dying, supporting a transmission ceremony that many of us close to Roshi couldn't participate in, because we were not ordained—with an entry into the outside world that was very different, sometimes very refreshing. I screamed and screamed at the Stones concert. There was a sea of people. I never loved Mick Jagger so much—in fact, in the old days I regarded him as sexist. That night I was with him totally—"I Can't Get No Satisfaction"—suddenly it was a great Buddhist song and there was Mick, fifty years old, prancing up on stage. He had survived. I loved my generation.

Being a cook those ten days was demanding. What did the Japanese eat? Each meal had to have three bowls of different food. I remember the steam on the kitchen windows—it was so hot in there, I was wearing tee-shirts—and the contrast of people coming in the back door, stomping the snow off their heavy boots, their faces red, their breath still fogging in front of their mouths. I entered the kitchen in the early morning dark and left in the dark of early evening.

At moments I caught glances of Roshi through the swinging doors that separated the kitchen from the zendo when he came down for maybe ten minutes a day for a certain part of the ceremony. He didn't look good. His face was deeply drawn and he was thin. I marvel now at his determination. When you're that sick, you rarely care about anything. He'd been through another round of radiation before the ceremony in the hope that it would stop the cancer, so he could be there even a little bit. He cared; he kept caring.

One morning I got tired of the fancy foods we were cooking. I was alone with no assistant for lunch prep. I thought, these are monks. I'll make them something simple, a monk's lunch. I baked whole potatoes with the skins on for the first bowl, steamed broccoli for the second bowl, and put some butter and chopped parsley into the third bowl for the potato in the first bowl. No fancy Japanese soy-ginger sauces or French cream sauces. A potato. Plunk in the bowl. American. Midwestern. I liked the aesthetic.

That night the visiting roshi lectured for the general public. I heard that he lectured about the potato served at lunch. "It is Dogen's food. Good, simple. The monasteries in Japan have become too fancy." I heard about that lecture the next day. I smiled. Katagiri Roshi was a Dogen scholar. Dogen was his beloved.

I did not go to the lectures at night, because I was too exhausted. Cary, too, was coming every day to Zen Center to help with the transmission ceremony. A while earlier, she had sewn monk robes in preparation for her ordination. Because of Roshi's illness, she was not able to be ordained by him. We would drag home together and sit in their living room, sipping Jack Daniels. Neither of us ever drank, but there we were, staring into space, glass in hand. The enormity of what was happening was too much to digest right then. Our teacher was dying. His lineage was being passed on. We were assistants, not part of it. Joni baked chocolate biscotti and we munched on them. I arrived in Minneapolis having not eaten sugar in two months, but my vow of no sugar fell apart during those ten days. Everything fell apart. There was no more wish in me, nor dream.

What Roshi worked so hard to bring to America was being formally transmitted that week. I heard he told Tomoe when he first moved to California: "I won't last long here. It is too hard, but the students in America are eager, serious."

What was hard? The language for one thing. English did not come easily to him. American culture, for another thing. It was very different from his native culture and he was being challenged to walk in Buddha's path of open-hearted acceptance in a very different world. Here is a poem he wrote for the twenty-fifth anniversary of *Wind Bell,* a Zen publication out of San Francisco Zen Center.

You are nearly as old as the number of years it has been
    since I came to America.
I have taught nothing to you at all.
I have done nothing for you at all.

But,
You have done a lot for me.

I can tell you one thing you have taught me;
    "Peel off your cultural skins,
    One by one,
    One after another,
    Again and again,
    And go on with your story."

How thick are the layers of cultural clothes I have
    already put on?
How would it be possible to tell a story without them?
How would it be possible to peel off the thick
    wallpaper

in my old house?
How would it be possible to ease my pain
whenever the paper is torn off?

If I were not to agree with your teaching,
Believe it or not,
My life would be drifting in space,
Like an astronaut separate from his ship
    without any connections.

Now I'm aware that I alone am in the vast
    openness
    of the sea
And cause the sea to be the sea.

Just swim.
Just swim.
Go on with your story.

Dainin Katagiri
(in *Wind Bell*, publication of the San Francisco
Zen Center, Fall 1986)

Recently I listened to a tape of Roshi lecturing. I was
amazed how difficult it was to understand him, how hard I had
to concentrate. In the years I was with him I grew used to his
English and after a while it was fluent for me. Hearing the tape
reminded me of how difficult it was for him. At the same time,
how deeply he understood me, Jewish-American from Long Island, feminist, writer, rebel with a hippie past. How hard he
worked to penetrate our culture. Yet, I think I wasn't unique or
so different. I was a human being. He understood human beings.

Suzuki Roshi once said to the early hippies who came to him in San Francisco: "With your dress and long hair and beads, you all look alike. I can't tell the difference. Shave your heads, get in black robes, and I can see your individual uniqueness."

My deep entry into Zen, into my uniqueness, another way of life, was through Roshi. He was dying. Cooking a whole day wasn't what drained me. It was what I wasn't doing, what I had no control of: his dying.

One morning, I had to carry a tray from the kitchen past the zendo to the inside porch. I saw the monks copying long scrolls. They called me over and showed me. The scrolls were the lineage papers. At the top was Shakyamuni Buddha and then a long list of eighty-nine descendants from Shakyamuni down finally, at the end of the long scroll, to "Old monk Dainin Katagiri confers on————"—then there was that blank at the end of each scroll where their individual Buddhist name would be filled in—"the lineage of Buddha." Zen was precise. The eighty-nine names listed were not abstract; not the Fifth Ancestor, followed by the Sixth. It was a list of specific Buddhist names. And my teacher was now on the list; he was conferring the lineage. He was passing it on. I heard that at a special ceremony—I was not in the building at the time—each monk mixed a drop of blood with Roshi's and their blood, mixed in ink, was drawn down the scroll, beginning at Shakyamuni's name and continuing through every name down to the two of them at the bottom and then back up again to complete the circle. This was how the monk entered the blood line of Buddha.

Seeing those lineage papers was the hardest moment of being excluded from the ceremony. Roshi was dying. I wanted to be bound to him that way. Blood was life. His life wouldn't be around long. I wanted to mix our lives. If only he was well enough, I thought. I could talk to him about it, tell him it wasn't fair. At least my protest would be heard; if he said no, I could accept it. But he was very sick. I had to accept it without speaking to him. I took a deep breath. I accepted it. I wanted to support him, but my heart ached.

That night when I went home with Cary, we spent a long time in the evening turning the pages of a big Georgia O'Keeffe book they had received as an early Christmas present. It was the one with O'Keeffe's flowers. Joni sat between us with the book on her lap and we sat on either side of her, eating another batch of chocolate biscotti.

"There," I'd point. "There is New Mexico," and in those pictures my state shone forth. The pink cliffs, the red hills, the bone-dry skulls. I wanted to take Joni and Cary there. It was a spot of light in the dark December landscape of Minnesota.

That night I realized there were thousands of descendants of the Buddha who did not get formal recognition on that scroll. So many people had passed through Zen Center, seen Roshi, loved him, remembered him, carried the seed. It was in all of us to sprout. I held that in my heart. I, too, am in the lineage of Roshi, I said to myself. I practiced with him. He taught me how to be a Buddha. I looked across the O'Keeffe book. Cary, too, I said to myself. In order to ensure the lineage, a lot of flowers have to be pollinated, not just twelve.

Then I remembered an old Zen story: A roshi was dying. All the monks eagerly gathered around the deathbed, hoping to be chosen as the next teacher.

The roshi said, "Where's the gardener?"

"The gardener?" everyone asked. He was just a simple man who tended the plants, not even ordained.

"Yes, he is the only one awake. He will be the next teacher," the roshi said.

Who wakes up is not who we expect. I felt a great responsibility: We all carry Roshi within us.

At the end of December, right before New Year's, I went to say good-bye to Roshi. I had to return to Taos. I had a writing workshop to teach there in January. He was lying on his side in bed under a blue cover, his hands under his cheek on the pillow. He could hardly talk; he was exhausted. I tried to make light talk. Then I was afraid I'd never see him again: I tried to tell him everything. It was silly; he was tired and sick. I got up after five minutes and said good-bye. He said, "I'll see you again." He had never said that to me before. I thought maybe he meant he was going to live. I hoped, maybe, but I knew he wasn't, not in the old way, not in his body.

The next day I got in my car and drove south through Iowa and into Kansas. I stayed overnight in Lawrence. Allen Ginsberg had written about that town in his poems. The next day Kansas spread itself in front of me. Brown hills and bare trees. In late afternoon, I blasted opera tapes that Joni had made me on my car stereo. I drove into Oklahoma and thought, how can a sky be bigger than this? I stayed overnight in a small town there and the next morning I entered New Mexico, its eastern border, and the sky was miraculously big, and, yes, there was a lot of space, but it was the quality of light that astounded me. It was golden, golden, golden, the way I'd seen it only in Jerusalem before. I knew I was home again and I was happy.

On Thursday, March 1, 1990, two months after I arrived home, Joni called me early in the morning to tell me Roshi had died that night. I had known since the past Sunday that his death was near, and I had planned to fly out that Thursday, hoping I would get there before he was gone. I didn't. I thanked Joni and got off the phone. I lay in bed for a long time thinking of nothing. Then I got dressed and packed. I drove the three hours to the Albuquerque airport, playing "Imagine" over and over on the car stereo, singing it aloud, very loud, with John Lennon.

I arrived in Minneapolis at ten P.M. and Teah, a Zen student from Tassajara Mountain Center, a monastery, picked me up and drove me straight to the zendo.

The night before, many of the Zen students had helped wash Roshi's body. Tomoe had generously insisted that Roshi felt that his disciples were his important children and should be present with the family for everything. Yvonne prepared the body with herbs to preserve it. She was one of Roshi's oldest students from the early days in San Francisco and had become a close friend of his family.

They wanted a simple pine box to place him in. They got one with a Jewish star on it. They took off the star and someone said, "Save it for Natalie." It was a star with a circle around it.

For three days, Roshi's body was in the zendo and we could sit with it at any time. By the time I arrived that night, it was the end of the first day. I bowed and walked into the zendo and went over to the open coffin. I was forty-two years old and somehow had managed never to see a corpse. This was the first. I stood and looked. The zendo was dark, except for lit candles at the altar. There were many flowers. Roshi's skin looked dark and dry and he didn't move. I just stood there. The windows near the body were opened and the cruel March

air of Minneapolis filled the space around him. I didn't believe
he was dead. I wanted to reach out and touch him, then shake
him. "Wake up, goddamn it!" I wanted to scream.

I sat down on a black cushion. The doan, the bell ringer,
was there for the evening, and Thomas, one of the Zen carpenters. The three of us sat. That's all. It was late. Lots of people
had gone home earlier. But I couldn't sit still. I kept thinking
I saw Roshi move. I adjusted my legs one way; then another
way. I moved my hands, my neck. Finally, I got up and went
into the kitchen. No one was there. I sat down at the kitchen
table and burst out crying. "I'd follow you any place, even if I
was a hundred miles behind, but now you've gone to a place I
can't find, a place I can't go." And I cried and cried until there
was no more crying in me that evening. I fingered the wood
table and then I stood up and went back into the zendo. I could
sit still now, and I sat with his body.

Late that night, I walked to Cary and Joni's along Lake
Calhoun. The ice was just breaking up in the lake and the snow
that wasn't melted was hard and dirty. Cigarette butts that had
lived under ice all winter were gathered in cement cracks. A
hard wind blew through my clothes and the sky was thick with
night clouds.

I dreamed that night that there was a closed mahogany
coffin with brass knobs standing all by itself out on a very green
lawn. There were no people, not even me. It was night and it
was pouring hard. The earth was very wet, rich and fertile.
Then the dream switched: My father picked me up in his white
Buick out in front of the airport. He was going to drive me to
the funeral. He said, "There's a big rain, but most of all up on
the mesa. It's wiping everything out up there." When he said
that, I saw a picture of my adobe house dissolving into mud,
except the center had a glowing light. I turned to look at my

father. I saw his big hands on the steering wheel. I turned my
head again. My mother was in the back seat. I saw her black
hair and dark eyes. She looked beautiful.

I woke from that dream at four A.M. In the dream, my
parents were carrying me to the funeral. My life had taken me
to this point, because of them. They had given me life. I carried
a lineage of strength. I had two fathers: One was standing in
the Buddha dharma and the other was the owner of the Aero
Tavern. My father and Roshi were two rivers converging inside
me. My father had said once when I told him about Zen, "I
fought the Japanese in World War II and now you're studying
religion with them." I turned over and fell asleep again.

The next morning I woke up with my heart aching; I
remembered why I was in Minnesota; I did not want to face
the day. I pulled on sweat pants and sneakers, left the house,
and ran hard down the cement sidewalk to Lake Harriet and
around the lake. I thought I could outrun pain. At the time, I
was in a track club in Santa Fe, training with a coach. I wanted
running to cure everything. It didn't, and though my heart was
pumping and I was breathing hard when I stopped, someone a
mile away wasn't breathing and his heart wasn't pumping, and
my heart ached because of that.

I went back to the house, showered, changed, went to the
zendo, and saw Roshi's body in daylight. His skin looked yel-
lower, tighter, his features were sharper—he was still dead. I
grimaced.

There were a lot of people sitting now, and some were in
the kitchen, preparing food. I stayed for two hours that morning
and then couldn't take it. I walked down to Calhoun Square
and wandered blindly in the shopping mall there. I couldn't
believe it, but I found myself purchasing a black leather book
bag that was on sale. I took it and almost dropped it in a garbage

can as I walked down the alleys back to Zen Center. I was in a complete daze. Luckily, after lunch Kate joined me. There was nothing to say. We just sat in front of the body.

The next day I brought a big tin of chocolates from Amsterdam and plunked them down on the kitchen counter. Bob, the man I had been dating, had arrived the night before from Europe and given them to me. Zen students, some who had been devoted to macrobiotics, all hovered around the tin and popped chocolates into their mouths. All of us felt a tension no words could express: Roshi was in the next room in a coffin.

On that third day, Roshi's skin began to shrink; his upper lip lifted from his bottom lip and I could see part of his teeth.

On Sunday morning there was a short ceremony at the zendo and then the coffin was closed and ceremoniously carried out by the monks to the hearse. Yvonne sat next to Tomoe in the black limousine. Tomoe looked out the window at the dismal gray landscape of broken ice, mud, and bare branches, and nodded at it. "That is how I felt when Roshi left for America."

I remember almost nothing at the cremation ceremony—who I drove with, what I wore—except that the service was in a room with a pink carpet, and that a Zen student who sat next to me was delighted her husband, not a Zen student, had surprised her and come. I remember only one of the several speeches that were given: It was by Erik Olson, a friend of Roshi's younger son, Ejyo. He told us what Roshi was like as his best friend's father: warm, playful, encouraging, a lot of fun. It was a beautiful speech; but I knew soon the body in that box would be burning.

The ceremony was over. The box was carried away by the

disciples. We all moved to a brown-carpeted waiting room, stood around, had tea, and visited with people we hadn't seen in a long time. After a while, Tomoe appeared. She was quiet, and there was a vulnerability about her. Yasuhiko, Roshi's older son, held his newborn son and sat next to his wife. As I brought the tea cup to my mouth, I felt as though my face had been ripped off.

Yvonne told me later that the crematorium allowed the monks to put the coffin in the oven, and she, Yvonne, in the presence of the disciples and Roshi's family, turned on the gas so the body would begin to burn. I walked down the street to Curran's with several of the Zen students. The restaurant was full of the Sunday church crowd. While we waited for a table, I watched cream pies move round and round on a rotating display case. When we finally were seated, I looked at the menu and there was nothing I wanted to eat. I ordered a plate of french fries. French fries! My teacher was burning and I was eating french fries. I remember they were the frozen kind. They were terrible and I ate them all with ketchup.

After we paid the bill, I walked back down Nicollet to the funeral home and went down to where the oven was. I walked down a long cement basement hall into a small cement room. The door was heavy and hard to open. It was hot in that room and there was a ferocious constant noise: It was the oven. Yvonne and two other people were there sitting zazen. I joined them as the body continued to burn. Fifty minutes before the cremation was finished—it takes five hours to burn the body completely—I opened the door of the oven and looked in. Through the heat and intense flames I saw two small ribs—that was all. They were the last of my great teacher.

. . .

Four days after the funeral, the day before I was to leave, I called Tomoe and told her I'd like to come by and say good-bye. We made an appointment for two in the afternoon. On my way there I stopped at Gelpe's, a special bakery on Hennepin Avenue, and picked up a beautiful raspberry cake. They put it in a white box for me, bound with string. I carried it up the stairs to Roshi's apartment and presented it to Tomoe.

She said, "Come, let's see if Roshi wants a piece," and she brought me into his study and placed it on his altar. There was a photo of him, leaning against a flower vase. "Go ahead, speak to him."

I knelt in front of the altar. "Roshi, I brought you a delicious cake. Raspberry. From Gelpe's. I hope you will enjoy it."

Then Tomoe and I went across the hall to the room where I last saw him alive. We knelt down at a low table and chatted.

"If he doesn't want the cake, later I will have a piece." She paused and then said, "Roshi once asked me, 'When you die, what do you want to come back as?' and I said, 'As a small white flower, like you see in a field.' He shook his head. 'That's so romantic. I will come back lifetime after lifetime as a monk.'"

I smiled at that, at his commitment beyond this lifetime.

The next morning I left Minnesota and flew to California to teach a writing and meditation workshop with Yvonne at Green Gulch Zen Center, a Zen retreat in Marin County. Roshi had taught there many times. I'd never been there before.

The first night I was there I had a dream: Roshi came to me and we walked along the gulch to the ocean. As we walked, we discussed different people I might marry; it was clear I needed to be married within six months. About one woman I brought up, he said, "Naa, she's too hysterical"; another man, he said, was too conservative. We stopped by some burned grass and just looked at it. Then he said, "But you know, that woman is also pretty wonderful." When we got to the beach, there was a snowstorm. Roshi stepped into the storm, turned around, waved good-bye to me, and then dissolved.

He said once in a lecture, "When I die, I die completely. There will be nothing left of me. It won't matter what you call me." And he said another time, "Don't cry when I die, go on."

Marriage was another commitment. Roshi was telling me in the dream to go on, to make another commitment, not to linger. I knew it was the only time he would visit my dreams. He had given me my instructions. I had to move on.

PART FIVE

I am here/now with your heart;
I hold your hands in here/now.

Dainin Katagiri Roshi

In June, three months after Roshi died, I went to Plum Village, near Bordeaux, France, where Thich Nhat Hanh, a Vietnamese Buddhist monk, lived and taught. I had seen a flyer hanging up at Zen Center that fall for this retreat, and several Zen students in Minnesota planned to go. I was the only one who finally ended up going. I'd read Thay's books (Thay means "teacher" in Vietnamese), but what really impressed me was a tape of him discussing the Heart Sutra. I listened to it one afternoon as I drove along the Rio Grande from Taos to Santa Fe. The Heart Sutra was that chant we did every day at Zen Center: "No eyes, no ears, no nose, no tongue, no body..." The chant that had stumped me, engaged me, entangled me, made me curious, full of wonder and laughter since my first days at Zen Center. Thich Nhat Hanh talked about it so simply, so beautifully. I wanted to meet him.

Plum Village was in the vineyard country. The zendo was a reconstructed three-hundred-year-old stone farmhouse. We slept on the floor on foam mats, three or four to a room. Meals were cooked on two burners in an open kitchen and we ate our meals silently, beneath a linden tree. There were only two daily sitting meditation sessions: one session early in the morning; and one in the evening before we went to sleep. That's all. It was very different from my Zen life in Minnesota.

Thay lectured every morning after breakfast and then we took a long meditation walk with him through the woods and fields. I liked being there. I was learning a whole new angle to Buddhism, less strict, less sitting, more walking, but in lectures

I had trouble paying attention, so I looked around me. People were busily taking notes. They obviously adored Thay. I liked him a lot, but I had just lost my teacher. I envied them for having one. Though I had "moved on" as Roshi had asked in the dream, it was only physically. My heart still ached for him, and with the kindness and slowed-down life of Plum Village, a question began to burn in me: Where can I find him now? I was sure the body we burned wasn't him. I was willing to climb down to Hades, if need be, to get him. Here—and then not here? It was impossible. Where did he go? I grew painfully determined to find him again.

I took long walks alone along the country roads, up and down steep hills, flanked by green grass and old, old vineyards, the crooked grape vines held up by long wires, the land here cultured and cared for, all of it. I sat in fields in the afternoon sun, writing in my notebook:

> A hundred thousand years will run through me before I can clearly say, Katagiri Roshi, black eye on a clear tin roof, I accept your death. I can say I will never forget you. I can say the vows I took I will carry into small towns in Kansas and Iowa, the yellow clover growing near the side of the road.
>
> Roshi, you know, there are a thousand things I never told you: My father owned a bar. I had skinny legs as a kid. My grandmother owned a poultry market and twisted the necks off chickens. They came from Russia. They spoke no English. Roshi, my father flew over Japan in World War II and dropped bombs over your small island country. I liked coffee ice cream as a kid and roast beef. My mother wore red lipstick and ate oreo cookies.

What was it like for you when you took your young wife to bed after green tea in the slow evening of Japan? Tell me now, what color were your school shoes and who did you love the best when you were eight?

A thousand things I will never know, but we walked that line, that dark deep one together and now I walk the roads of southern France, but you are not here. I'm going to find you again. I promise. I won't be left behind as you walked over to the other side, someplace I can't see, a place so thick with gray I thought the air turned into an army of planes. My great teacher, sometimes now I want to relive your death, grab your body from the flames and run off with you. I'm afraid you're gone for a long time, longer than I expected, and I won't find your face again in this lifetime.

(notebook entry, June 1990)

I walked in the heat of one afternoon to a thousand-year-old stone church and sat in the cool of it and heard even my breath echo in its stillness. It was lined outside by cypress trees and there was one white pigeon by the well.

Sometimes I'd skip evening meditation and sit in a vineyard and watch the sun set over a hill. It seemed to set differently there. The sun would flame orange and round in a pale white sky and then descend over the horizon. No color after or around it, unlike New Mexico. And then a while later darkness would come, and stars. It felt complete and I watched the whole thing.

Then sometimes in the evening after everyone else left the zendo, I'd go in there and sit a while, knowing there was yellow clover out the window, and in the morning, bees. When, Roshi, when? I'd think to myself. When will I see you again? Death seemed an impossibility. I couldn't comprehend it. He said he'd see me again the last time I spoke to him. "When"—I wanted to scream at the trees through the zendo window—"when will I see you again?" And then I'd take my legs out of their crossed position, bend my head on my knees and sob. Hard, quickly, direct. No holding back.

Every Wednesday at Plum Village, we had Lazy Day, a whole day to completely relax. On one Wednesday near the end of the month, my friend Jim and I did walking meditation on a small country road to a French town six miles away. We stopped and watched a machine attached to a tractor collect hay in a field and then emit it out the back as a golden roll, like a fresh loaf of bread. We were so slowed down by the time we reached the village that we sat down on a stone bench in a church courtyard for a long time, watching a bee in a red rose, and felt, yes, this was enough. This was everything.

On the way back we munched a dark chocolate called Noire, meaning "black" in English, which was seventy percent cocoa.

"Stop, Jim," I said as we headed back, and we sat for a half hour by a pond, watching a swan glide across the water.

One day in the last week, at six A.M. twenty of us had tea with Thay in the zendo. At last, I thought, I'll get to ask my question.

Linden tea, dried from the tree outside, was served, and cookies were passed around. Thay asked us, "How do you connect with community?" and we began to his left, each person taking a turn for a few minutes to answer his question. I was the fourteenth to go. I stepped right through protocol. I did not answer his question. This was my only chance to ask him.

"Thay," I said, "my teacher, Katagiri Roshi, died four months ago. I studied with him for twelve years. I miss him very much." I paused. My voice cracked. "Where can I find my teacher now?"

"I knew Katagiri," he said. "He was a great man. For two summers, I invited him to Plum Village. He could not make it." He nodded his head. "He made it here this summer. You can find him here. In the trees. In the birds. He's here now."

I nodded. "Thank you," I said. I looked down. We went on to the next person. I took a sip of tea. I knew what he said was right, but I also knew I was not ready for it. I wanted the man, the human being. I wasn't ready to let go.

I did find him again, eight months later.

Heartsick over the Gulf War, I'd wake up in the mornings crying, and I'd think to myself, what do I know about peace? I had a lover then, and we fought all the time. We were waging our own private war and if it wasn't the two of us, there were many times a day when I'd feel aggression or anger or desire about one thing or another. And now here it was on a large scale. We were destroying a country.

After the war had been going on for two weeks, I woke up one morning and said, "Okay, Nat, what are you gonna do? Think! What can you do? You've had all those years of practice, what are you going to do? Pick one thing and do it under all circumstances, like Roshi taught you."

I made a sign with the help of a friend: Sitting for Peace

in the Middle East. Please join us. Every noon to twelve-thirty, weekdays. It was nonpartisan. I didn't say someone was good or bad, right or wrong. We were sitting for peace. No one could argue with peace. I made the sign on a Saturday. That Monday, I would begin. A young writer, Rob Wilder, whom I'd met a few weeks before, heard about it and said he'd like to join me.

On that Monday, he met me at 11:30 at the Galisteo Newsstand, where I was writing. Together we walked over to the Santa Fe World Travel Agency. The women there were my travel agents and they had generously given me permission to leave the sign, which was large and cumbersome, nailed to a long pole, and my meditation zafu and zabuton there every day in their basement, so we could easily pick them up and walk the half block to the plaza, which was in the center of downtown Santa Fe. I carried the sign, Rob carried the black cushions, and we walked slowly down the sidewalk. Some pedestrians turned their heads. A teenager gave us the peace sign.

We came to the corner and crossed the street. The plaza has a center, and then radiating out from that are sections of grass and trees flanked by sidewalk. We chose a section with two benches facing each other and cement in between. I placed my zabuton and zafu down on the cement, took off my shoes, bowed to the cushion, and sat down, cross-legged. Rob leaned the sign against the bench and sat down on the bench with his shoulder leaning against the sign to steady it. About four friends joined us and sat on the benches. I took a traveling clock out of my jacket pocket, placed it on the ground, and marked a half hour with it.

It was February. A cold day. It all opened in front of me: all those years of practice. I could sit still under any circumstance. I felt the steadiness of that zazen position, the power of that foundation. I thought if some madman came by and kicked me in the teeth, I would not budge and it was not from willpower.

It was from the magnitude of the simple sitting position I took and all the years of practice echoing at my back. I was amazed. I'd learned how to do something in that zendo. What? To do nothing with no ripples, causing no trouble. To sit still. And I felt everything backing me: the trees, the birds, the sky.

In front of me, I could see the dry, yellow winter grass and pigeons, fat ones, pecking at seeds that bypassers threw. The pigeons were beautiful, gray and white, orange, yellow. I breathed in and out. The shadows of bare branches crossed in front of us and bent over us. They moved from my left to my right, but slowly, ever so slowly, marking the sun's movement. We were all connected from way out there in the solar system to here where my foot was getting cold.

The clock said half past twelve. I bowed and said, "May all beings be peaceful," and stretched out my legs. People stirred on the two benches. Rob and I carried the sign and cushions back to the travel agency. The women at the agency were eager to know how it went. The first day was finished, Monday, February fourth.

I couldn't have imagined how hard it would be to commit myself to one thin sliver of a half hour in the middle of the day. I changed airplane flights so I would leave after twelve-thirty on Fridays, and returned early Monday morning to make the sitting at noon, after driving the hour from the airport in Albuquerque. I had to rearrange my life.

One day I was in the middle of negotiations with my realtor for a house I was buying. I was excited. I'd been looking for a house for a year and a half and I thought I had one. I looked at my clock: ten minutes to noon. It was hard to tear myself away. Oh, maybe I could just skip today. What does it matter? Few people join us. Go, Nat, said another voice. Go. In a split second, I turned, took a deep breath, felt a little foolish when I said, "Joan,

I'm sorry, I have to go sit for peace in the plaza. I'll meet you again at one," and I dashed off, skidding to the zafu at noon. Rob had already picked it up with the sign. He had never sat prior to the plaza sittings but his commitment was true. I got in position and we sat. It rained that noon, hard. Rob and I were the only ones there. No pigeons, no casual passersby. I watched the rain hit the sidewalk and bounce. My hair was sopping wet, so was my jacket. I was happy to be there, that beautiful, peaceful half hour in the middle of the day. "Make positive effort for the good," Roshi told me after my divorce. Every day Rob and I were doing that. No matter how crazy I felt in the morning, stirred by the last night's dream or my morning's writing, everything turned when I sat on that zafu outside under trees and sky. I watched how big time was: A half hour was tremendous. How long it took—I could hear the shoe steps—for a person to walk from the statue to the street, across my path. How enormous the rain was with its small hands.

When I met Joan, the realtor, at one, she said, "You know, while you sat, I went and had a bowl of soup. I never stop in the middle of my day to eat. It was really nice. Thanks." We both smiled.

There were days when one or two of the Santa Fe crazies who hang out on the plaza joined us. One sat next to Rob with a big boom box on his lap blasting, "I left my Chevy on the levee," and trying to talk to me. I sat still. Should I say something? In a moment, I turned to him: "We're silent now. Later we'll talk." I turned my head back. He sat a few moments more and then wandered off. One man sat still for ten minutes, said, "Man, I can't do this any longer," left, and returned at the end for five minutes. Two tourists, who didn't know each other, sat down at 12:05. The woman from New York began a discussion about peace with the man. She gave her precise opinion of the Vietnam War. Again I turned: "We can talk later. Please let's just sit now."

"Oh, I can't do that," and she trailed off. The man scratched his ear and followed her. An old man with a wool hat said one day, "I'll show you how to get real peace," and he handed us a photocopied page from the Bible.

Three secretaries brought lunches and sat on a bench across from us and discussed their boss. "Oh, I saw a bottle in his lower left-hand drawer." They giggled.

Many times Rob and I sat alone. One day it snowed. The pigeons looked beautiful through the white flakes. There was a fat gray one that always seemed to lag behind and miss the thrown popcorn. He scurried to another place and was shut out there, too.

I bought a journal made of recycled paper and bound in black cloth with white Japanese calligraphy on it. It became our sitting journal. Rob and I wrote in it each day:

February 26th, 6 people
Nat, Rob, a college guy, a woman who wanted to talk about peace, not sit for it, Bev and the guy in black, who plays his radio and sang for us. Weird day, full of energy. It was warm and the people came and went and the guy in black sang to us on his bike in front of Nat. I saw Nat almost begin to laugh as he sang. The guy has a picture of a teenage girl on his box.

(Rob)

I got a cold on top of my cold and wasn't going to sit. Walked to the Galisteo this morning and it was freezing out. Had a great talk with Kate on phone

this morning. I feel lost and found. Just trying to
hang out in the life I've got. I'm good and doing fine.

(Nat)

A photo of us sitting was taken for *The Reporter*; a German
video team taped us one day. Two poems kept going through
my head when I sat. One a third-grader in Minneapolis had
written years ago:

> Chicken and the car won't go
> Spells Chicago
> Smells pretty good.

And one by Raymond Carver that I had memorized, the last in
his book written when he was dying of cancer:

> And did you get what
> you wanted from this life, even so?
> I did.
> And what did you want?
> To call myself beloved, to feel myself
> beloved on the earth.

("Late Fragment" from
A New Path to the Waterfall,
Atlantic Monthly Press, 1989)

And one day it seemed to bubble up from the very earth
I sat on—I heard Roshi's words. Words he'd repeated often in
his lectures, but that I had paid little attention to before. Now
I heard them: "Peace is not a matter of discussion. Shut up and,
like the Buddha, sit down under the old tree." Peace is not

something to fight over. I heard his words. I heard them. He was with me again. In my ribs and chest and lungs and face and hair. I carried him in me. He was sitting with me and with the trees and birds. It was so simple.

Yet there was a day in April when I was walking down Palace Avenue in Santa Fe—the war was over, at least officially, it was warm out, I wore a blue cotton dress, I was swinging my arms, happy—when a thought came to me: I sure would like to have tea with Roshi one more time.

I stood at the corner. I was quiet. The thought went through me again. I'd give anything to have tea with him just one more time. Then I stopped: Was I serious?

Well, what would you give? I asked myself. Would you give up your new house in Santa Fe?

I nodded, yes, in a second.

What about your heart's home on the mesa?

Absolutely. To see Roshi again? For sure.

What about your success?

I'd give that up.

Okay, how about your two published books?

In a snap. I was feeling exuberant. I thought I was going to get to see him.

Now the real test: I asked myself, Natalie, would you give up your writing?

I paused. And got very still. Would you give up your writing? The question fell down through my body.

Yes, to have tea with Roshi one more time, I'd give up my writing. Yes, I'd do that.

I knew it was true. I meant it. I felt a great freedom sweep through me.

Well, then what would you do if you didn't have writing? I answered slowly: I'd walk these streets. I'd look at the leaves and the no-leaves in winter. I'd sit still at bus stops and feel my breath entering my body. I'd bow to trees. He'd be with me in sunlight and in the cold blue shadows of winter. I'd have him always in a new way, without doing anything. I'd live like a monk, bringing everything I know into nothing, not holding on to anything.

Couldn't you do that and be a writer, too?

Maybe so, but at this moment on the corner of Palace Avenue, just having tea seems awfully sweet.

LOOK FOR NATALIE GOLDBERG'S NEW BOOK

LIVING COLOR

A WRITER PAINTS HER WORLD

Natalie Goldberg's acclaimed books on writing have set hundreds of thousands of readers free to explore their own creativity. Now she reveals one of her own secret sources — the wildly colorful paintings that are her "underground stream of mayhem, joy, nonsense, absurdity."

"Natalie Goldberg paints as she writes — with a passionate, singular vision. Part memoir and pure magic, Living Color *is a book of luminous humanity."*
— Julia Cameron, author of *The Artist's Way* and *The Vein of Gold*

"Natalie Goldberg is a magician. Seeing the world through her eyes, each of us becomes an artist at living and being — a wondrous feat."
—Sue Bender, author of *Everyday Sacred* and *Plain & Simple*

More than sixty brilliant full-color reproductions of the author's distinctive and joyous paintings appear throughout.

A Bantam Trade Paperback
On Sale September 1997

AN 2 8/97